Life on the Lickey
1943-1986

Pat Wallace

BREWIN BOOKS

BREWIN BOOKS
56 Alcester Road,
Studley,
Warwickshire,
B80 7LG
www.brewinbooks.com

Published by Brewin Books 2014

Reprinted June 2014

A CIP catalogue record for this book is available from the British Library.

ISBN: 978-1-85858-523-9

Printed and bound in Great Britain
by 4edge Ltd.

Contents

Introduction 7

Acknowledgments 8

Brief History of the Lickey Incline 9

Patrick John Wallace 11

    Engine Cleaner 14

    Bank Links 1947 17

1947: A Hard Winter 19

    Winter Over 24

    Station Terrace 28

1948 33

    Nationalisation 33

    The Army years 34

Back on the Railway 36

    1950 36

    1951 40

    Number 1 Link 41

    1952 43

    Fire Cleaning 45

    Fire Cleaning on 2290/58100 46

    1953 46

    No 1 Link 47

    1954 49

    Exam Questions 50

    1955 54

    1956 58

    Taking 58100 to Derby. 7th May 1956 59

A footplate ride up the Bank 61

1957 64

The Salto 66

1958 66

1959 69

1960-64 71

Standing Second 74

Diesel years 81

Drivers and firemen after shed closed 83

Diesel Hydraulics 92

1969 Roster 98

Trains booked bankers in 1969 100

Oil Leak 101

Another Oil Leak 102

Roster from 1-2-1972 104

Accident at Eckington 109

Last Day 111

End 112

Introduction

23rd January 2013, a snowy day but nice to sit in the warm and start a record of my life on the Lickey. When the depot at Bromsgrove closed in 1986 I did say that I might write a book and it is a pity I have left it so long but here goes. I have all my diaries somewhere to help me if I can find them; I'll need them as my memory is not what it used to be.

After a search I managed to find the diaries that I was looking for, the first one is 1947. This is the neatest of my diaries and was written with a Parker 51 pen which my mother had bought me for Christmas. The diaries continue until 1959 when I stopped for some reason but they will enable me to recall some of the most interesting times, the jobs I worked, the locos and the men that I worked with. From 1960 onwards it will be a case of racking my brains and enlisting the help of other Bromsgrove railwaymen.

Acknowledgments

I WOULD like to thank the following for their help in producing this book: Ian Tipper, Darryl Lucas, Richard Gibbon, Mick Wood, Barry Troth, Eric Underhill, Bob Dunn, Gordon & Joan Russell, Alan Spencer, Sid Usher, Phil Marshman, Keith Hargreaves, David Houghton, Charles Berwick, Chris Fox, Paul Troth, Roger Carpenter, Pat James, Michael Mensing, R.M. Casserley and Neil Gordon.

Brief History of the Lickey Incline

WHEN I started at Bromsgrove the railway had been open for over a hundred years. The line from Cheltenham to Bromsgrove was opened in June 1840 and the Lickey section as far as Cofton a few months later on 17th September. From Bromsgrove to Blackwell the line is dead straight and climbs at one in thirty seven point seven for just over two miles. The line had been surveyed by William Scarth Moorsom after Brunel's route was deemed to be too long. Originally stationary engines were to be used but there were some engines being built in America which were supposed to be good hill climbers and so some were ordered.

These engines were built at the Norris Locomotive Works in Philadelphia. They turned out not to be that good. They were designed to burn wood but in this country they had to burn coke so as not to make any smoke. The cast iron fireboxes soon had to be changed for copper ones too.

Initially a bank engine would couple on the front of a train and assist to Blackwell. Later, after some of the engines had been converted to saddle tanks by James McConnell, the train engine would be replaced by a banker which would take the train to Blackwell on its own before being replaced again at Blackwell. This was later changed to two engines on the front as earlier.

When James McConnell became the locomotive engineer he had a special engine built at Bromsgrove just for banking. This was a saddle tank called Great Britain and was a great success.

The Midland Railway later took over the line and some better engines were introduced. All the American engines were gone by about 1856.

Nobody seems to know an exact date but trains eventually started to be banked from the rear.

In 1914 designs were drawn up for a large engine to bank trains up the Lickey. The war intervened however and it didn't finally emerge from Derby Works for its first test run until January 1st 1920. This was the famous engine usually known as Big Bertha but to us as the Big-un. Her arrival at Bromsgrove was reported in the 7th February 1920 edition of The Messenger calling her a Leviathan and saying she was expected to do the work of two engines.

The situation from then until I started remained pretty constant with this one big engine and up to half a dozen 0-6-0 tanks commonly called Jinties being used for banking. Sometimes a 3F 0-6-0 tender engine was used as well.

Patrick John Wallace

I WAS born on 31st December 1929 at 6, Ford Rd, Bromsgrove and was the eldest of three children having a brother David and sister Doreen. We lived at Ford Road until after the war when we moved to Fox Lane. Dad bought the land at auction and had a house built, I remember there was a shortage of London Bricks and there was a delay in building the house. Our old house still continued its association with railways as it was bought by Bromsgrove fireman Royston Cummings.

I went to school at St Peters Roman Catholic and then Watt Close when I was 11. I did alright at school but was never good enough to think about going to university or anything so when the time came for me to leave I had to get a job.

I wasn't afraid of work and from about the age of 10 I used to help Tom Gower with the hatching of his chicks and also help him to pick his Codling apples. I did some work as well for Mr Lacey who had a place up Rock Hill; I would help with the harnessing of the horses which he used for ploughing and scuffling. I would also help my dad as he had four allotments and kept pigs, chickens and rabbits. At Christmas all our relations would come round and we would gather round the piano and sing, we had lots of relations as my dad was one of eleven and mum one of six.

This was probably where my love of music came from and when I was about twelve or thirteen I started to have music lessons. Once a week on a Sunday morning I would go to the house of John Longmire who lived off the Stoke Road. Mr Longmire was music master at Bromsgrove County High School. Here I would go through my scales and sometimes play a John Ireland sea shanty. The two Johns were best friends and had lived together in Guernsey before escaping to England before the Germans invaded.

My Dad had worked for the Midland Railway (LMS) at the Carriage and Wagon Works at Bromsgrove for many years and thinking ahead he got me an interview for a job on the railway. This was about 6 months before I was due to leave school. I notice in my diary that I sometimes recorded Bromsgrove Rovers results this was probably because my Dad was a footballer and played for Aston Villa and for Bromsgrove Rovers; he was as hard as nails. He said I wouldn't make a footballer as I was too soft. I think working on the railway toughened me up a bit, at least physically.

I don't know whether my Dad thought it was better working on the Loco side or whether there were no vacancies at the Wagon Works but the interview was with the Bromsgrove Shedmaster Mr Brookes. Also In attendance was Miss Rudge, Daphne; she was a clerk and daughter of Bromsgrove driver Les. I remember going up the stairs to the office and sitting at a desk and being asked various questions; I can't remember what they were now. I couldn't start until I was 14 but I had my name on the books.

It was a kind of apprenticeship as you might say if you wanted to become an engine driver you had to start at the bottom. I started as a bar boy on my 14th birthday 31st Dec 1943 as you couldn't be a cleaner until 14½. I started work at 8-00am as you were not allowed to work shifts at 14, and I finished at 4-00pm. I Had a Vindec bike to go to work on from my home at 6, Ford Rd and as it was wartime I had to carry a gas mask with me at all times.

It was about a mile and a half to the shed and it took me about ten minutes. This was before all the houses were built at Charford and my journey was down a narrow country lane past farm buildings and on to the Stoke Road. I was under a chap called Horace Pedley who travelled from Worcester and was a boiler smith. Ted Spencer who was a fitter would also be working on the engine and his assistant was a lady called Gladys. Now what bar boys used to do was this. I had to go into the firebox feet first with 20lbs of steam still on the clock and any burnt fire bars I would have to push through the ash pan into the pit. Then the other job I had to do was, you had a long pair of tongs and you had to put new fire bars in place of the ones I had removed. Some of the bars slipped in easy but some were hard. I was only a slip of a lad and the combined weight of tongs and fire bar was probably more than my weight. The other end of the loco was what was called the smokebox and then my job under supervision of the boilersmith was to rod the tubes so they were all clear. As well as rodding a steam lance was connected to the loco and the steam pressure left in the boiler was used to blow out the tubes. If there was a bad blockage sometimes you had a terrific backdraught and my face would be covered in soot, it was a horrible job. The boilersmith had the job of tapping the stays to see if they were broken. We had half a dozen or so small tank engines at Bromsgrove, some 2F or 3F tender engines and the famous Big Bertha and I worked on all of these.

There were some other young lads working as bar boys and I remember John Rudge and Gordon Baker. I went to school with John and Gordon. John started shortly after me but Gordon had started some months before. Besides them there were lots of cleaners whose names I have forgotten. Looking at my diary for 1947 it says that I was a bar boy for six months, an engine cleaner for two years and a passed cleaner for 5 months. The shed cabin was at the entrance to number 2 road and was used by the cleaners, bar boys and other shed staff such as Arthur White who was the steam raiser. Above it was the shed master's office. There were some open wooden stairs leading to the upstairs office and a big sink with a cold water tap underneath it.

The shed had three roads each with a pit and number one and three had ash pits outside but not number two; number one was a through road. At the rear of number 2 was the fitter's pen and the stores were at the rear of number 3. It was at the stores where you booked on duty at a small hatch where you were given your brass check which you kept until the end of your shift when it was handed back. In the stores were shelves containing spare parts and some big tanks containing oil. Cotton waste and cloths were also kept here. There was a desk where drivers could fill out their timesheets and a glass fronted case on the wall which contained notices. There was a sand drier at the rear of number two. Sand was shovelled in the hopper at the top and after being heated came out dry enough for use in the engine sandboxes. This hot sand which had a distinctive smell was kept in a wooden bin between the two entries from number two to number three roads. Wet sand and bales of cotton waste were kept in a little place just inside number three road.

Engine Cleaner

As a cleaner I worked three shifts. On the six till two shift there were about twenty of us. The two till ten shift had about eight and on nights just two. On days most of us would be cleaning the engines which we did with a mixture of paraffin and cleaning oil. It was a really dirty job and my mother used to ask me what on earth I had been doing when I got home in a filthy state. There was a lot of fooling around amongst the cleaners with oily rags flying around so it was impossible to keep clean. The rest would be doing other jobs such as coaling engines. This was a hard job but helped to build you up ready for firing. There was no proper coal stage at the shed and the engine would be placed next to a wagon of coal. The coal would be shovelled from the top of the wagon to start with and when the level had gone down a bit the door of the wagon would be opened and propped up by a hefty piece of wood. You would then stand on this and shovel the coal into the bunker or tender.

During the war years all the engines had side sheets so the glare from the fire couldn't be seen from above. They also had their cabside numbers blacked out. I can remember when war broke out as each year we had a week's holiday in Morecambe and we were on our way back home on the train when we heard the news. We would sometimes get ambulance trains coming through taking the injured to Selly Oak and the Americans would throw out packets of Chesterfield and Camel cigarettes and gum. We also had ambulance trains bringing wounded to Bromsgrove.

When I became a cleaner I had a rise in pay. I'm not sure how much this was but I think I would have only been on about £2 a week. Being a cleaner entailed using the shed bike and going to drivers and fireman's houses, this was known as knocking-up this was done on the night shift and entailed calling at the houses of all the drivers and fireman that were required to book on between the hours of one and six. Knocking on peoples doors at that time of night meant we didn't usually get a very good reception. The bike was a big heavy thing painted black all over because of the war; it had no gears and was hard going but I was not allowed to use my own. Most of the drivers and firemen lived in Aston Fields, so we didn't have to go too far, Sidemoor was probably the furthest we went and we never went out of Bromsgrove. As it was wartime there were no lights I think I only had a small light on the bike. The third job I did as a cleaner was working with Tom Riley on the water softening plant. I remember Tom for bringing big doorsteps of bread for his dinner with a piece of cheese and an onion, he had this every day. There were three different sorts of additives required for the process and we would have to carry these heavy bags up the steps to the top. Caustic Soda and Lime were two of them, I think and maybe Rock Alum was the third. The water was treated in this way to make it softer and reduce scale and prolong boiler life. Round the back of the shed by the water softening plant was an old tender where all the sludge went. When it was full it went away on the Salto to Washwood Heath and then on to Derby to be emptied before being sent back. Cyril Bedford and Tom Goode also worked on the water softening plant at one time.

When I was a cleaner we had a lot of suicides down the Old Road (Stoke Works to Abbotswood via Dunhampstead) and we had to scrape all sorts off the undersides of the engines. The police would go down there and collect up the remains and put them in a casket. An engine would then run through the section before it could be reopened.

I was put in charge of eight Italian prisoners of war and they would be given instructions to load a six or eight planker wagon with ashes. These men only worked down the south and not at the shed. They were very handy with their hands and would gather willow from some trees by Garringtons factory and make baskets. I had a couple of them for my mum. Although it was wartime and a time of rationing these men always seemed to be well provided for. Every day they always had the same, a giant tin of pilchards and loaf of bread. Two of them had good voices and would sing opera; I loved this as music was my passion. These men would arrive for work in the back of a lorry, from Droitwich, I think.

I don't remember too many bombs being dropped on Bromsgrove but we did see some dog fights overhead. John Rudge and I went over the station one day; we got our jack-knives out and dug bullets out of the platform wall. We had them made into cigarette lighters at a shop in town.

Lord Haw Haw, one of the announcers on the radio station Germany Calling once said "we are not bothered about bombing Bromsgrove because they are a lot of imbeciles and lunatics". Very nice!

The nearest air raid shelter to our house was behind the Drury Works in Worcester Road where my mother worked and to get there we had to cross the Spadesbourne by planks. It would get very crowded in there with everyone squashed together.

My dad was too old for the army but he was in the Home Guard, Captain Ryland was in charge in Bromsgrove. The Ryland Centre was named after him. In November 1940 Coventry was badly bombed and my dad, along with hundreds of other workers from the wagon works, was taken to Coventry to help with the clear up.

One of the most thrilling experiences I had when I was a cleaner, it was either VE day, 8th May 1945 or VJ day in August when I had permission to put detonators on the straight on both rails and run over them. I think it made the local newspaper The Messenger.

By Dec 31 1945 I had worked at the shed for two years and now that I was 16 I could be made a passed cleaner and have my first firing turn. The most senior passed cleaner would be used first it was all done on seniority. Becoming passed out also meant a rise in pay but I don't remember how much. As a passed cleaner I had jobs on the bank and also what were called control relief jobs to Gloucester or Birmingham or possibly to Derby or Burton. Most drivers only signed to Birmingham or Gloucester I don't remember my first job it but it must have been a relief when it was out of the way and I knew I was going to make it as a fireman. I was only a passed cleaner for five months before a vacancy occurred and being the senior boy I was promoted to fireman. This meant more pay again.

April 1st 1946 found me travelling to Derby for an eyesight test which I passed and on 27th May I was made fireman and had regular firing turns. As a passed cleaner I had 135 firing turns so I must have been firing practically every day. My first experience of being derailed was during this time when I was working with Jim Roberts, we came off the road at Tunnel Junction, Worcester as we were about to go on shed.

My first diary starts on 1st Jan 1947 so who my first driver was as a fireman or what engine I don't remember. I remember working on a number of American engines which I thought were very ugly. This was probably after the war in 1946 when I was a passed cleaner. I don't remember my driver's name but I do remember relieving Gloucester men on the up goods and they spent a lot of time explaining the workings of the engine and where all the controls were. I only worked on these a few times and they must have been alright once you got used to them as I don't remember having any problems.

I was firing in the bank links for 18 months then in the mainline links from Tuesday 5 August 1947. These links were groups of turns that you progressed through as your seniority increased. We had four links at this time with about a dozen jobs in each plus a small link with just a couple of jobs shunting the Carriage and Wagon works. The first men I remember on the Wagon Works shunter were driver Alf Griffiths and Jack Adams was his fireman. Jack was a permanent fireman and probably failed his eyesight test. 3130 was the engine used for shunting at this time and I remember the brake which was a brass handle in the centre above the firehole which you turned before saying your prayers, it was not very good. The other 2F 3099 was used on the Salto, Night Goods or Ashchurch pick-up. These engines were later replaced by 3F's. Everything was done on seniority on the railway from the day you started and it was a slow progress to eventually be a driver in the top link.

Bank Links 1947

These are the booking on times in the bank links, we would have gone through the links booking on at these times in the order they are here. Sometimes we would swap turns with another fireman or perhaps your regular driver would swap. All these jobs would have had turn numbers. Unless it says otherwise the jobs would have been on a tank engine although sometimes a tender engine would be substituted. When we booked on the driver was allowed 10 minutes to read the notices to see if there were any speed restrictions or other alterations which may affect him, we then had 10 minutes allowance to walk to the ash pit. If you were on the ash pit then the men being relieved would have 10 minutes to walk back to the cabin and the driver another 5 minutes to fill in his time sheet.

Bank Link booking on times 1947

4-05pm	1-30pm	8-45pm
4-45am	12-05am	12-45pm
10-15pm	2-15pm	12-05am on 2290
8-05am	6-15am	3-00pm
4-05pm on 2290	9-30pm	7-00am
1-00am	5-30am	11-00pm
8-05am 2290		

As you can see we booked on at all times of the day and night.

1947: A Hard Winter

1ST JANUARY 1947 was a Wednesday and I booked on at 7am with Arthur Laight. Arthur came to Bromsgrove from Redditch and came to work on his motorbike. He lived up to his name and was often late. Arthur was at Bromsgrove for a number of years before returning to Redditch, he would sometimes bring some of his children to work in his motorbike and sidecar and I remember they were very well behaved. Two of his sons, Gerald and Terry later joined him on the railway as firemen at Redditch. Our engine was 7303 which we did 4 trips with and then we were relieved at 3-45 giving us 45 minutes overtime. This might not seem a lot of work but it would have included cleaning the fire for which we were allowed about 45 minutes. While the fireman was cleaning the fire the driver would be going round the engine doing the oiling. The other thing to remember was that for every ton of coal that was shovelled into the firebox the same amount had to be put back into the bunker or tender down at the coal stage, the water would have been topped up after every trip too except on the Big-un where you could do two or three trips.

All this coal had to be replaced on the coal stage and for this there were coal men working round the clock. Some I remember are Ray Wardle known as Doc, Pop Liddell, Mick O'Neil, Harry Bartlet as well as Tom Goode and Gilbert Field who did the job sometimes. I think Tom was born in Gloucester but had lived in Bromsgrove for many years by the station in one of the railway houses. Gilbert Field lived further away at Uplands off the Birmingham Road. As the Big-un used more coal the coalman helped with the coaling of this engine, but not with the Jinties.

I was with Arthur for the next three days on the same engine and we did 4 trips each day, my wages for the week were £4-0-2d.

The 5th of January was a Sunday and I booked on at 4-05pm. Our engine was 2290 known as Big Bertha or to us as just the Big-un. My mate was A.W. Bates (Walter) and we did two trips. Walt, as we usually called him, was one of those drivers who were always impeccably dressed. His hat was polished as were his shoes and also his hand lamp. There were still the odd goods about on a Sunday but mainly passenger and so there were fewer engines out on a Sunday. I have recorded "1 in fire relief K. Stokes". This would mean that one trip was done since the fire was cleaned and my relief was K. Stokes. When I was a cleaner I had heard about ringing the bell and had asked what this was. Apparently on the Big-un if you managed to throw some coal right down the front it made a ringing sound as it hit the front of the firebox, you weren't a proper fireman unless you could do this.

The next week I started on the Monday (6th) with Dennis Lott on 7276. Dennis was a smashing chap who had come to Bromsgrove from Bristol. He was a tall chap over 6ft and was one of our younger drivers. He lived up Finstall Rd. opposite the rugby club in a bungalow. Dennis was very religious and never swore, unlike some of our other drivers. It was very sad when Dennis died while still in his thirties. We booked on at 4-05pm and did 4 trips. I did not work with Dennis too many times before he died. This day was when we had the first fall of snow of that winter and it would have been a bit tricky riding my bike.

The next three days I was with Walter Bates, known as Basher, on 7276 doing 4 trips each day. The snow had turned to rain on the 7th and then finally cleared, we didn't know at that time what was in store for us. Nothing out of the ordinary happened except on the Thursday at 9-40pm there was a track failure on the up and down lines. Probably someone ran through a light engine to see if it would clear, it usually did. Friday was a change as still with Walter we had 3604 and 7303 and did 5 trips.

The Saturday brought a change of mate as I was with Frank Newsome. Frank was an old driver who was a bit round shouldered which made him look shorter than he was. You could tell Frank was not a local from his accent he had come to Bromsgrove from Blackpool and he lodged in Worcester Street by the Turk pub. 4 trips again.

My earnings for the week were £5-1-2d.

Monday to Saturday 13-18 I was with Harry Marsh, Harry lived in Newton Rd and walked with a limp after a railway accident when a loco ran over his foot, I also remember Harry kept pigs in his garden and because of this was sometimes referred to as Hoggy. Harry smoked a foul smelling tobacco which he said was herbal. We booked on at 4-45am and had 7301 for the first two days then 7443 with the number of trips varying between 3 and 6. On the Thursday (16th) there were 12 trains on the block at Kings Norton and only two goods trains went up the bank between 9am and 2pm. Wages for the week £4-1-10d.

The following week it was on nights booking on at 10-15pm with Walter Bates again with either 7313 or 7303 all week and doing 4 or 5 trips. On the Wednesday 22nd the snow started again and although I didn't record it in my diary we had weeks of snow and freezing conditions with the snow drifting up to the windowsills of the upper floor of houses. With the snow as bad as it was there was no way I could ride my bike so it was shanks' pony every day. At the water column down at the South and at the station there were braziers to stop the water freezing.

Before starting on nights this week with Walter I had my first music lesson on the Monday at 3-30pm with Miss De'ath. I should have had a lesson each week but with the weather the way it was they were often cancelled. Miss De'ath had a studio at St Johns House by the 48 steps which led up to the church; I think she was French or Belgian.

It was a change of driver on the Saturday as I was with Bert Moyle, Oiley Moylie as he was known, Bert lived in Sidemoor but originally came from Wales he was a clever man and made beautiful models of railway engines. Eventually Bert failed his eyesight test and ended his time working on the shed. We only did 2 trips and had an early finish at 5am.

The following week was a bit of a mixture as I was with Ted Guy on the Monday on Control Relief, booking on at 8-05am. I'm not sure what happened that day as just the engine number is given, 3423. Ted lived in Piano Row, Aston Fields. He was later to fail with his eyesight and was put on the Carriage and Wagon shunter. Ted injured his hand one day when oiling the side rods and the engine moved.

Next day I was on shed duties booking on at 5am which must have been nice, all that snow on the ground. This would have entailed preparing and disposing of about five or six engines. Disposing of an engine would have meant me clearing all of the clinker out and most of the fire, just leaving a bit under the door. If the engine was due to be washed out then the firebox would have been emptied completely. Hopefully the fire would have been run down and there would not have been too much to do. The ash pan would have to be raked out and the smokebox emptied of char.

For the fireman preparing an engine meant building the fire up ready to leave shed, checking the injectors, making sure there was a shovel, tools, detonators, and bucket and hand brush. The tools would be a number of different sized spanners and the largest of these was the 7/8th. This was sometimes used when the clack valve on top of the boiler stuck and being the biggest and heaviest would be used to give it a clout. The clack valve was what admitted water into the boiler. The lamps would be filled and trimmed including a gauge lamp. A check would be made to make sure the coal was stacked correctly and there was no danger of any falling off. The smoke box door would be checked to make sure it was tight. An important job on the bank was also to check the sand boxes were full and that they worked. Inside the shed there was plenty of sand that had been heated in the sand dryer but it was a hard job lifting it up to the running plate to fill all the boxes. The driver would be going round the engine to check everything was in order and doing all the oiling. We were allowed about 45 minutes for preparing a Tankie and about an hour and half for 2290.

On the Wednesday, 29th, I was back on the bank with Ted Allen, known as Monty, and booked on at 8-05. We had 7303 for one trip then changed for something a bit bigger, 2290. We did three trips with the Big-un before getting relieved at 4-25pm. Monty was a smashing chap to work with, I think he came from the LNWR at Walsall or Monument Lane, I remember he was very tall and had a moustache. The other thing I remember was that he was a horse racing fanatic and loved to have a bet. In later years his regular job was on the Wagon Works shunter.

I should have been on at 8-05 the next day but my diary says that I had the flu. It must have been 24hr flu as I was back at work the following day. Perhaps I didn't want to go out in all that snow.

The temperature was not rising above freezing in the daytime and we were having more snow but I was back at work on the 31st, a Friday. I booked on at 10-30am Control Relief with Ted Jeffrey. We had locos 3838 and 3550 I don't know where we went but we made 40 minutes overtime. Ted was another nice man and he shared my passion for music and played the piano, he lived in Dragoon Fields, Aston Fields.

The following day I was with Ted again booking on at the same time with engine 3340. Again I don't know where we got to but we didn't get relieved until midnight giving us 5½ hours overtime. It must have been lovely trudging home that night. I would have been able to have a lie in the next morning though as I was not due to book on until 4-05pm with Ted again. We were on the bank with 7303 and did 4 trips and got relieved at twenty five minutes past midnight.

I should have been on 4-05pm bank on 2290 for the rest of the week but I swapped with K Stokes for 6-00pm extra Bank. Whether this was my idea or his I don't remember but it would have certainly been easier on a Jinty than the Big-un. Having said this I see I finished the week working on control jobs with 4049 and 4232 on the Friday and 4049 and 3946 on the Saturday. These were Saltley engines except for 4232 which was from Canklow.

The weather was still bitterly cold this week with snow falling nearly every day and strong winds. The next week instead of finishing in the early hours I was starting at 1-00am, this was the start of seven days with Sid Hollingshead. The weather was still bitterly cold with freezing fog on some days. The railway must have come nearly to a standstill in the second part of the week as we didn't bank any trains on the Thursday or Friday and only one on the Saturday. When a lot of snow was expected a snow plough would be fitted to an engine, one of the tender engines I think, by fitter Ted Spencer. I remember down the Old Road between Dunhampstead and Spetchley it was very open and the snow would be drifted across the line. The first time I went down there with the snow plough I remember being very apprehensive as we hit the snow and progressively slowed down. We then had to reverse and take another run at it. I remember going on the snowplough about five times altogether. Eric Underhill remembers a Standard class 5 coming down from Saltley and he fitted the tube blower off the 0-10-0 to it and spent a couple of days perched on the front of it de-icing and de-snowing the points from Stoke Works to Barnt Green.

The third week in February I was with Walter Bates again and things must have started to get moving again as we did four or five trips each day. This was on an afternoon shift booking on at 1-30pm.

A note in my diary does say though that the first mail was 110 minutes late. It was normally due about 9-20pm.

March started off with some sunshine and no more snow for the first three days but all this changed with blizzard conditions on the 4th. It was probably because of this that my mate Walter Bates didn't arrive for work until 4-00pm on the 5th as his train was late. He should have booked on at 2-15pm. I was on the same engine, 7301, all week, Monday to Saturday, with Walter. Also on the Wednesday the 3-59 up express didn't arrive until 9-10pm.

Sunday March 16th was a day off but we had a terrific gale which started in the late evening and lasted for almost 11 hours. The following week it was wet and very windy every day. I was on nights with Walter, booking on at 9-30pm, so it probably wasn't very pleasant. Cleaning the smoke box, not a nice job at the best of times, would have been made much worse by the wind blowing the dust in your eyes. There was some shelter at the coal stage but the coal dust could still be blown back at you as you filled the bunker. 7313 was our engine for five out of the six days and the last day Saturday we had 7301. We did 24 trips that week.

Winter Over

With the snow rapidly melting there were floods everywhere but at least I was able to get to work on my bike again. It was an early start for the next six days; 6-30am with Driver Donald McHarg, known to everyone as Mac. Mac lived in St Godwalds Lane opposite the tennis club. He always appeared to me to be very nervous but he was very meticulous and when he was relieved the engine would be in good shape with all the oiling done properly. I think that Mac came to Bromsgrove from Monument Lane but had worked at other sheds too. This week we were on 7313 or 7301. The next day, a Sunday meant I could have a lie in as it was an 8-05 start on

2290 with Mac again. The following week with Walter on 7301 took me to 100 firing turns on Good Friday 4th April.

Having worked on Good Friday I had the Monday off before resuming with Walter on the 12-45 shift with 7565. Winter seemed to be over and my diary records the first day of sunshine on the Wednesday. 2290 was not out that week so there was probably an extra Jinty. For a washout she would have only been out of action for a day so what was the problem? Was she on shed, at Bromsgrove, Saltley, Gloucester or maybe Derby?

We did 22 trips in five days with this engine and it would have been hard work. 7565 was fitted with a bigger Jimmy than the other Jinties and so burnt a lot more coal, it would be throwing it out of the chimney and I remember putting my head out on one occasion and getting some down my neck. Not to be recommended. For those who don't know, a Jimmy was a device that was fitted to the blast pipe to increase the draught and so produce more steam. This was against the rules as more coal was burnt but I think a blind eye was turned. The firebars were closer together on 7565 and this may be the reason why she had a bigger Jimmy. I think the only tank engine not to have a Jimmy was 7276 as this seemed to steam well without one.

The following week I was booked on nights at 12-05am with 2290 but the Big-un must have still been out of action as I was on 7313 all week with Walter. I was also booked to work on the Sunday, 12-05 on 2290 but my mate didn't show and my diary says I was on shed duties. My mate should have been Sid Goodway.

This was budget week and cigarettes were a shilling for twenty and tobacco one shilling and two pence. I don't think I smoked much in those days so it wouldn't have affected me too much.

My turn the next week was with Walter again on 3pm Bank with 7443 but we took her to shed on the first day, Monday 21st, with a broken axlebox and bent side rod. Our replacement was the hungry 7565.

Nothing of note happened the following week when I was on early mornings 3-35am on the Monday followed by 4-45am the rest of the week with Frank Cliff. Frank was another one that came from Monument Lane; he lived at Churchfields and rode to work on his bike.

Some drivers that I worked with in the following weeks that I have not mentioned so far were A.T. Newman (Tom), Doug Miller, Harvey Haylings, B. Baulch and Sid Wheeley. Tom was a smashing chap, very quiet and reserved although at Union meetings he made sure he had his say and got his point across. Tom lived up Stoney Hill and kept racing pigeons as did Sid Wheeley. Harvey Haylings was a big tall chap and friend of Sid Wheeley. Billy Baulch was a little round faced chap and very pleasant to work with, he was another one that came from Monument Lane.

I think Doug, Harvey and Sid all had about the same seniority and came from the LNWR. I think Doug and Sid were also on the S&D at Bath Green Park. It was very sad when Doug passed away in the mid-sixties when only middle aged.

The first week in June I was with Walt again on nights, booking on at 10-15pm on 7273. On the Friday we left Bromsgrove at 1-55am but stuck at the Blackwell distant signal. We waited there for forty minutes before another banker or two came to our assistance and we finally arrived at Blackwell at 3-15am. If you were struggling and didn't think you were going to make it to the top it was always wise to stop here before the train was on the catch points just short of the summit.

Two more drivers that I worked with in June were Sid Hollingshead and T. H. Field (Tom), Tom had come from Saltley and I think Sid had once been at the Midland shed at Worcester. Sid tended to drive the engines hard but would also help you fill the firebox with lumps.

The new summer passenger timetable started on 16th June and I was back on 2290 for a few days.

A new rate of pay started this month and I was on 93/6d per week. At the end of the month I was with a different driver again, booking on at 1-30pm on the Sunday with Sid Wheeley and doing four trips with 7308. Sid was another one that lived locally in Aston Fields and would walk to work down through the goods yard. He later bought a van and would sometimes come in that if the weather was bad.

It was quite busy on the bank in July with all the passenger trains and we were doing five or six trips as normal. I had some back pay this month too and my wages were £14-5-9d one week.

The name W. Hardy (Bill) appeared in my diary for the first time on Sunday 13th July when I worked with Bill on 12-05am with 7425. Bill was a driver who always came to work looking very smart with his boots polished and his grease top hat too. He had two sons and like a lot of railwaymen lived in Stoke Rd opposite to the entrance to the goods yard. I think Bill came to Bromsgrove from Bristol

Five or six trips continued to be the norm through July and I did my 200th firing turn with Walter on 7425 on the 30th.

On the 5th August I started a period of Control Relief jobs, the first being with George Stanley. With these jobs we booked on at the shed and waited in the cabin for the phone to ring and tell us what job we had. Some of these jobs were easier than others it depended on a lot of things. First of all was your driver and how he worked the engine, then there was the condition of the engine, the fire could be full of clinker and unlike on the bank you would not have the best coal. Sometimes we had what were called briquettes which were just compressed coal dust and pitch. These were about a foot long and six or seven inches wide and deep, a smack with the hammer and they would break into four nice pieces. They had the name of the manufacturer on them, Crown Works, Cardiff. Nothing was moving very fast in those days and we would spend a lot of time just waiting for a signal to clear or the train in front to move. In this situation it was a case of keeping the engine quiet but being able to get steam quickly when needed.

We were booked off on the Monday as it was a Bank holiday but we started at 11-30am on the Tuesday. We worked to Exchange Sidings and although we never worked back we still made over an hours overtime. It was very congested in the Birmingham area and this was a regular occurrence. Sometimes we never made it that far as the rest of the week we were relieved at Lawley St, Duddeston Rd and Kings Norton. On the Tuesday my diary states 6 hours from Stoke Works to Bromsgrove so perhaps we had a long wait in the cabin for our train. Most of the engines were 3F or 4F but this week we had two 8F's, 8313 and 8606 so perhaps these were heavy trains. 4576 and 4591 were the other two we had that week. George and I finished off the week doing five trips on the bank with 7639 on the Saturday.

I was with George again the following week on 1-00am Control Relief. The first day or night should I say we booked on at 12-05am and went light engine to Saltley with 4553 which was a Bristol Barrow Road engine. The next three nights we made it to Water Orton and then Washwood Heath on the Friday. 2753, a Crab was our engine on the Tuesday. This engine was shedded at Agecroft so was a long way from home. These were usually good engines and when control gave me the number of our engine and it was a Crab I was pleased. They had a funny little round seat and being good steamers you would usually have time to sit on it.

On Saturday 16th August I must have left George sitting in the cabin as I was with a Saltley driver whose fireman had been injured. We went as far as Cheltenham with 3265 before returning on the cushions. Being on nights this week was probably quite welcome as the summer of 1947 was very hot.

It was back on the bank on the Sunday with George Dyer though we only did one trip with 7313. George lived in a railway house next to the station.

Station Terrace

Station Terrace was a row of houses built by the Birmingham and Gloucester Railway Company for its workers when the line was built in 1840. Next to George Dyer lived the Berwick family with Charles Senior working at the shed and Charles Junior a fireman a few years older than me. Also living here were the Goode family, Tom and Ada and driver Danny Stainton. These houses might have been the height of luxury when they were built but with only gas lighting and no running water they had seen better days. Water was available from one of two taps for the whole row and the washing was done in one of the two brew houses on a designated day of the week. Toilets were shared by three or four families, all this for seven shillings a week. These houses got the nickname Bug Row when eighteen children had Scarlet Fever and were taken to Hill Top Isolation Hospital. On another occasion a number of children developed Diphtheria.

We didn't get too many Black Fives but I had two the next week, 5447, a Saltley engine to Washwood Heath with George Stanley on the Tuesday and 5274, a Bescot engine, from Worcester to Washwood Heath on the

Saturday. My diary states "Washwood Heath, over" so this probably means we pushed the train in front of us over the top so the wagons could be directed into their correct roads for forwarding. We then usually took our engine to Saltley shed where we disposed and then made our way home. This usually meant walking to Vauxhall station and getting a train to New St and then another ride on the cushions to Bromsgrove. If we couldn't catch a train we sometimes went to New Street on the bus or walked which took about half an hour.

Even when booked on Control Relief it didn't mean working on the main line every day as the next week proved. I started on the bank for two hours on 7425 before going on shed duties for the rest of the shift. After this it was two trips to Washwood Heath and one to Cheltenham before having another hour on the bank on the Saturday and then shed duties. All this was on nights with a 10-00pm start.

This is how the rest of the year went working all over with different engines and drivers.

I should have been 6pm Control Relief starting September 8th but my mate, George Stanley, was on holiday and so I was on the 1-30pm bank job firing 7638 with three different drivers, Vic Randall, Jim Core and G. Muddiman. Vic Randall came to us from Crewe and was another who lived up Finstall in one of the bungalows. Jim Core was born in Bromsgrove but I think he had moved around a bit before coming back to Bromsgrove and later becoming Shedmaster. He had two brothers who were also drivers at Worcester. I can't remember anything about G. Muddiman; I don't think he was with us for long. We managed 31 trips in six days.

I spent most of my mates 2nd week's holiday on the bank with Les Rudge and 2290. Les was a Bromsgrove man but had spent some time at Crewe before coming home.

At the end of September the Big-un was renumbered as when I was with Frank Cliff on the 29th it had changed to 22290, this was because the number was needed for some Fairburn tank engines being built at Derby.

Some of our drivers signed further than Birmingham and this was the case with Jim Core. In October I was with him for a week and we went to

Burton twice making four or five hours overtime each time. One of these jobs was with one of my favourite class of engines Crab 2875. This week also included trips to Lawley St, Landor St and working on the bank. I wasn't too keen coming back passenger with Jim as he believed in communism and would often get in heated arguments with people, it was best not to mention politics around Jim. On the engine he would sit reading the Morning Star newspaper.

On the 20th I went to Washwood Heath with Sid Goodway on Canklow 8F 8407 before having a go on an S & D engine 13805 light engine. This engine was probably on its way back home to Bath Green Park after a visit to Derby Works.

Most of our main line jobs seemed to take us north but I finished off the month with three jobs to Gloucester and one to Cheltenham with Crabs, 3F's and 4F's.

Joe Clapton is a driver I have not mentioned yet but I was with him on 8th November 8-05am bank. We were on the Big-un and did five trips. You could tell Joe was from Worcester as he spoke with a very broad Worcester accent, he came to Bromsgrove for a while and then went back. He was a very experienced driver and used to drive the compounds on the Birmingham to Worcester trains.

There was a block failure at Bromsgrove on the 15th but it must have soon been sorted as I did five trips on 7313 with Walter. I seemed to work a lot on this engine and it was different to the others as the cab was painted with a wood grain affect. I am told that this was once a Somerset and Dorset engine so perhaps this is why the cab was painted so. I worked on other S & D engines but don't remember whether they were the same.

Starting on 18th (my 300th firing turn) I had four days on the Ashchurch pick-up with a 3F. For this job we booked on at 8-08am. I didn't work the Friday as I had my army medical which I passed grade 1. My driver for the week was W. Phelps (Bill). Our first job was to deliver some water to the crossing keeper at Oddingly and throw some coal off and then we used to shunt at Defford, Eckington and Ashchurch. This was a good job to be on as at Ashchurch there was a large brick food store called the Provender Store and during a break in shunting we would be given a number of tins of food each. The tins had no labels on and we used to shake them and try to guess what was inside. The tins would usually contain fruit, peaches, apricots or pears but we sometimes ended up with peas. We would work back to Bromsgrove with the same engine this would have been quite easy as we didn't usually have too many wagons on. When we arrived at Bromsgrove we would put the train inside and go to shed.

We didn't usually have Control Relief jobs on a Sunday but on Sunday 30th November I had a job with Doug Miller to Landor St. This was a place we were often relieved as it was near the shed at Saltley and a set of men would walk over to relieve us while we took water. If we had been on duty for many hours we would go back home passenger or we may be asked to work another train to Washwood Heath or Water Orton. Whether we did this depended on the driver and whether he was one that liked to make some overtime.

Earlier in the week I had a Super D 9377 on a job to Up Sidings with my regular mate George Stanley. I liked these engines as they were powerful and usually steamed very well and it was a pity we didn't have them more often. Some of my drivers that had come from the LNWR, such as George, were very familiar with them and gave me some tips. A thin fire was all that was needed if you had some half decent coal. The injectors were a bit strange as you couldn't look out of the cab to see the overflow pipe as it was under the cab and so it was a case of listening to see if it was working right. These engines would often work down on a Bamfurlong to Stoke Gifford train which conveyed coal to Stapleton Road Gasworks.

Sid Usher remembers an unusual engine around 1947 when he started. Tom Newman and Sid Wheeley worked an LNWR engine north from Bromsgrove. Queen of the Netherlands was the name Sid remembers but it is a long time ago so it was possibly Prince of Wales class Queen of the Belgians. Unfortunately neither Sid nor Tom are around to ask.

Wilf Vallender was my mate when I had a Sunday afternoon job on the bank (4-05pm) with 7303 and 22290. Wilf lived in Newton Rd not far from George Pidgeon. He loved to watch the wrestling on the television and would dash home on a Saturday afternoon so as not to miss it. He unfortunately had a heart attack at the end of August 1963 when he was only 52 and died. I had been working with him earlier that day on the bank and dropped him off at his house on my way home.

The week before Christmas it went very quiet and I only did 15 trips in six days. On five of those six days we had two engines our first one probably having to go to shed for washout. There was an engine washed out each day which meant that they were all done about once a fortnight.

A new rate of pay had started on the 4th, 104/- per week.

The weather was a bit different to last year and there was no white Christmas. I had four days off before resuming work on the 29th on shed duties with George for four days, 3am start. The last fall of snow for the year was on the 29th. No doubt we would have had a good fire going in the cabin. Engines dealt with in those four days were, 3210 21A, 7234 21C, 3379 18B, 3492, 3621 21A, 22290 21C, 7305 21C, and 7276 21A, some more than once of course. 21C was Bromsgrove, 21A Saltley from where we would often borrow engines and 18B was Westhouses. The Westhouses engine may have been a failure on the main line or just been on Saltley shed when we requested an engine. The fourth day was New Year's Day 1948.

During 1947 my first full year of firing I recorded working on 93 different engines. This meant Firing for 28 different drivers both on the bank and main line and I would have gained a lot of experience.

With some of my diaries on 23rd January 2013 and about to start writing this book.

2290 as she was originally before the tender was cut down to aid coaling. Author's collection.

Bromsgrove shed 4-5-1949. Apart from the concrete in front of the engine this was how it looked when I started in 1943. H. C. Casserley courtesy of R M Casserley.

The Garringtons shunter taking wagons into the factory in 1949, our loco coal wagons and cabin on right. Newton farm is in the distance with the social club still to be built. Author's collection.

2290 with steam reverser but otherwise as I first knew her with headlamp and cut down tender.
D M Newband. Author's collection.

2290 as she was when new, probably 1920. She is pictured on the up line at Blackwell. Roger Carpenter.

7234 shunting in the up yard, 26-3-49. Norman Glover.

Arthur Laight walking towards the camera in 1954. On the Jinty is Frank Cliff. The man on the right is Hereford Bill Lewis who was a welder at the wagon works. Photographer Unknown. RR597 Author's collection.

Not as much snow as in 1947 but it gives you an idea of the Lickey in the snow. 15-2-1960. R J Sellick.

7238 standing first by the exit signal from the bank engine siding. The driver is possibly Vic Randall. Author's collection.

2290 at Bromsgrove in 1935. Photomatic.

Looking smart in my new uniform having joined the army in 1948. Author's collection.

48331 passes the coal stage in 1949 with a down freight, 69999 and a Jinty rest between duties. Roger Carpenter.

47565 on shed at Bromsgrove. Author's collection.

2P number 530 at Blackwell on a local passenger 13-5-50. R S Carpenter Photos.

41053 starting from Blackwell with a local passenger train. Joe Moss courtesy of Roger Carpenter.

45597 near Vigo in July 1957. Copyright R S Carpenter.

A quiet time at the South in 1951. Author's collection.

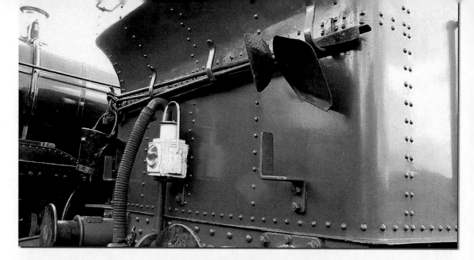

A selection of fireirons and clinker shovel. They weren't usually as straight as these. Phil Marshman.

From top to bottom, Pricker, Clinker shovel and Dart. Ian Tipper.

Eric Underhill used the knowledge he had gained as a fireman to become an expert model maker after he left the railway. He is shown here with one of his Big Bertha models. Ian Tipper.

58100 on the ash pit at Bromsgrove South. This was where we cleaned the fire. Author's collection.

Cooking a few bangers on the shovel. This is on Worcester Locomotive Society loco 5786 (L92) at Totnes. Albert Jakeman would cook his breakfast on the shovel while coming down the bank. Ian Tipper.

Walschaerts valve gear on 58100. Author's collection.

An up express double headed at Vigo in July 1957. Copyright R S Carpenter.

69999 passing Kings Norton in 1955. The late Ted Higgins.

Ted Higgins on right, signalman at Blackwell in 1942. Ted was signalman at Blackwell, Bromsgrove, Barnt Green and Kings Norton. I would often chat to Ted when we were stopped at Kings Norton and also Edgar Limerick.

7436 assisting a Black Five at Blackwell and probably going as far as New St. She was not one of our regular engines and is carrying a 21A shedplate so is probably on loan to us. Locomotive and General courtesy of Roger Carpenter.

92008 returning through Bromsgrove station after banking the 4-45pm Bristol-York up to Blackwell. 17-8-1955, 7-03pm. Note the concrete supports for Wagon Works traverser, water tank at rear of shed and steps for station staff on down platform. There is a train waiting on up goods and what looks like enthusiasts on the up platform. Michael Mensing 46-4.

Caledonian Pug 56020 at the rear of Bromsgrove shed 21-6-53. This engine was replaced by another Pug 51217. R B Trollope. Courtesy of Roger Carpenter.

The backhead of 58100 on what is thought to be its last day of service. Author's collection.

The replacement for 58100, number 92079, complete with headlamp and tender cut out. Seen here with 5226 assisting a freight at Vigo. Eddie Johnson collection.

This was possibly taken in 1949 when O S Nock paid a visit to Bromsgrove and rode on 58100 with Ron Stokes and also had a trip on a Jinty. I have read his article in Railways magazine and he appeared impressed with the work of the bankers. P B Whitehouse on left, O S Nock in centre. P J Garland courtesy of Roger Carpenter.

1948

Nationalisation

THE RAILWAYS were nationalised on 1st January 1948 and we were all now working for British Railways. All our engine numbers were changed, 22290 became 58100 and most of the Midland engines gained a four before their number but it was a long time before this was completed and most men still used the original number.

The first full week in 1948 I was with Jack Bishop booking on at 3-55pm to shunt the Wagon Works. As well as shunting the wagon works we would go down to Stoke Works with some wagons of coal and shunt there. Returning to Bromsgrove we would make the train up for the night goods and later get relieved by the 11-55pm men which meant we booked off at about 12-20am. The 11-55pm job was in the bank link whereas the 3-55pm and 7-45am were in a little shunting link. Although we had drivers that didn't drink Jack Bishop wasn't one of them and if there was a pub nearby and time to spare Jack would be in there. He would encourage all the young firemen to drink and if you tried to keep up with him you would end up drunk. Jack had once worked at the Midland shed at Worcester. We had 7234 all week. Finishing the week with a Sunday job with Wilf Vallender 7am extra bank and then a ballast job, this was with locos 7303 and 7313. I should have been 3-43pm control relief starting on the 19th but I was with Edward Stone known as Ted on 6pm bank.

The 1st of February made it three Sundays out of four when I was on 4-05pm bank with Sam Smith. This would have been a quiet time as my driver was known as Silent Sam because he rarely spoke; it may have had something to do with the fact that he was the only man at the depot that was not in a union. After starting off with 7276 we swapped it for 7305 and only did one trip. Sam was very economical and didn't seem to want to open the regulator, there was no fear of your fire going up the chimney with him and only a thin fire was needed.

Harry Hinett seemed to be my regular mate for 1948 (you changed mates every year) and although my diary says "Railway work slack everywhere" we seemed to have had a job every day on control relief. With 4553 on the 25th we waited 50 minutes for a banker while working to Up Sidings and it took 25 minutes to climb the bank, probably the result of not having enough bankers. We never worked back but made 4hrs overtime; this was probably because we spent so much time around Kings Norton where trains would queue up one behind another. Eric Underhill remembers spending so much time here that they ran out of water and he had to throw the fire out. In the cold weather when we had stopped behind another train we would often join the guard in his brake van as it was warmer than staying on the engine. In foggy weather the guard would have put detonators behind his train and even though we were waiting for them they still made you jump.

I had a pay rise in March when my rate went up to 107/- per week.

On Friday April 2nd I was on the 12-10pm with Harry Hinett but before going to work the postman arrived with my army papers.

My final job on the railway before starting National Service was on Friday 9th April when Harry and I booked on at 3am Control Relief and worked to Landor St with 4272. We booked off at 10-50am and that was it for a couple of years.

The Army years

I went to Catterick for my initial training before being sent to join the Royal Corps of Signals at Pocklington where I spent all my time on a disused airfield. Pocklington was in the west riding of Yorkshire. I was an Orderly Clerk which was actually the colonel's private secretary. I worked in the Orderly Room and had a number of Clerks under me. I was typing letters and dealing with secret, top secret, confidential and restricted documents. Some of these documents had to be sealed with wax and sent by despatch rider. Lieutenant Colonel C. P. S. Denham-Young OBE MC was in charge and his second in command was Major Weeks. As my work was important it would sometimes get me out of parades. I enjoyed my time in the army and made some good friends some of whom I am still in touch with today. I still remember my pay number 6606401.

On 2nd February 1950 my army life came to an end and I set off from York at 9-15 for Kings Cross arriving at 1-15pm. I made my way across London to Waterloo where I caught a train to Aldershot. This was where everyone had to go to be demobbed. I got to Aldershot at 3pm and it couldn't have taken too long as I was at Euston for the 6-55pm train arriving at New St at 9-10pm. I remember when I got home that my Mum had a big plate of food waiting for me. I had a lie in in the morning until 10-30 as I was tired after all that travelling.

I decided to treat myself when I returned from the army and bought a new Hercules bike for £16, a new suit for £7, and a raincoat which cost £4-17-0d.

On the 6th of February I went down to the railway and arranged to start work on the 13th. Mr Brookes had departed by now and Tug Wilson was in charge.

Back on the Railway

1950

WHILE I was away in the army some new faces had arrived but the biggest change at Bromsgrove was the arrival of the Garratt, 69999. I wasn't to work on this giant too many times as it moved away before too long. It had a massive firebox, 57sq ft. and burnt a huge amount of coal. If you did manage to fill the box and get a good head of steam it was a tremendously powerful engine but everyone was glad when it went away. Some said that with this engine you didn't need a shovel but a wheelbarrow and plank. Another problem with this engine was the brake, it was so slow to act and you had to be very careful going out behind a train. Passenger trains were only booked to stop for a minute or two for a banker and you didn't want to have time booked against you.

I started back with the driver I had finished with, Harry Hinett, a 7am job to Saltley carriage sidings with 44411, a 4F which my diary says was a good engine. The way to fire these engines was to keep the back of the box well filled and nothing much under the arch. If you put too much under the brick arch they wouldn't steam. The engines I had the next two days 47565 and 44262 were also good and it was just as well as I had a bad cold.

The next few weeks were just as before my army days with jobs on the main line to the Birmingham area or Worcester with Harry. Harry had come to Bromsgrove from Bristol and would tell me about firing the Devonian from Bristol to Leeds where he would lodge for the night and then work the southbound Devonian the next day. He probably came to Bromsgrove to get his driving job.

On 13th March I was with Jack Smith an elderly driver on the shunter booking on at 7-45am. The rest of the week I was with Jim Roberts on Birmingham jobs. Jim lived close to me in Brook Rd and his nickname was Chesty. His wife was very friendly with my mother and they were both members of the WRVS and were into jam making, knitting and gardening. This didn't make Jim any friendlier with me however and like every other fireman I was still not allowed over his side of the footplate.

After having a week off in March with flu I had a few days on the bank with Harry, only the second time on the bank since 1948. I wonder whether I phoned in sick or just never showed. We didn't have a phone at home but I had the number of the loco in my diary, Bromsgrove 2750.

My first time on the Big-un for over two years was on 17th April with Harry 1-05am doing two trips. This was a Monday morning and was one of the quieter shifts as goods trains from Wales and the south west wouldn't start until after midnight and it would be a few hours before they reached us. On quiet shifts like this the chance would be taken to have a game of cards in the cabin, Misère was a popular game at the time but we played all sorts.

We had a change of scenery at the beginning of May when we went to Gloucester twice and Cheltenham once with the usual 3 and 4F's. Later in the month I had a whole week on the bank with Frank Newsome. An unusual engine turned up on 6th June when I was with Bert Moyle. 2P's were not very powerful engines and were normally to be found on passenger trains but when we booked on at 9am we were told our engine was 40523 a 2P 4-4-0 shedded at Gloucester Barnwood. This was probably not a very heavy train and we worked as far as Lawley St.

Starting on the 26th of June I had five out of six days on the bank, the first two with Wilf Vallender on the Big-un and then two on 47308 with my own mate Harry. On the Friday I went up in the world when I was called upon to work with Worcester driver Joe Clapton on the compounds. He was known as Yorky Joe and like the other Midland drivers at Worcester, was very experienced and could get the best out of these engines. He had very rosy cheeks, spoke with a broad Worcester accent and was another one that wore a flat cap instead of the regulation grease top. These passenger trains were normally worked by compounds and on this day we had 41073 and 41030. I don't remember having any problems on these jobs and as passenger engines they were probably well looked after and had the best coal. These drivers were very experienced with them; they started off in simple before going on to compound which made them very economical. There was not usually any overtime on these passenger jobs as they normally ran to time and I booked off at 9pm. The reason we had this passenger job was that there were two drivers, Charlie Trigg and Ted Love at Worcester and one fireman, by the name of Thomson I think, so we had to cover the other fireman's job. These men were all that was left from when Worcester had a Midland shed which had closed in 1932. The remaining men now came under Bromsgrove.

On this job I booked on at 2-30pm and travelled passenger to Worcester where I met up with my driver. We would relieve a set of men in the bay at Shrub Hill and work all stations to Gloucester. These would be Norton, Wadborough, Defford, Eckington, Bredon, Ashchurch, Cheltenham and Churchdown. We would be relieved at Gloucester Eastgate and wait for a Bristol to Birmingham train which we would relieve before working back to Worcester. At Shrub Hill we were relieved by some Bournville men. My driver would then go home leaving me to go back on the cushions to Bromsgrove.

I was back down to earth the next day on the bank with Harry and 47308.

Ted Stone was my mate on Saturday 8th July booking on at 1am and working to Up Sidings with Saltley's 43949.

Although I was in the top link, number one, I was on the bank for three weeks in July and August. As well as my own mate I was with Trevor Gwynne for five days then Wilf Panting on the Saturday. Trevor had been at Bromsgrove for some years and he and Wilf were big pals. Wilf used to have shares in the railway company and I remember when we had the cabin fire banked up with coal he would take some off saying that we were wasting company coal. Wilf's father was also an engine driver. Another week I was with Ted Jeffrey. We were probably short of men some being on holiday. Ted was a nice chap who I enjoyed working with. I was with Vic Maund on 18th July working to Castle Bromwich Bay with 44151. This was the only time I remember working with Vic, he was an old driver and I remember he would sit in the cabin with a fag in his hand and fall asleep, when the cigarette burnt down he would wake with a start. Vic lived next to Bob Gill in New Rd Aston Fields. Wilf Panting also lived in the same row. All these road names will mean nothing to anyone that doesn't know Bromsgrove but it just shows how Aston Fields had become a proper little railway town at that time as there were also many who worked at the wagon works, goods yd., station, signal boxes and permanent way. If you worked on the Loco side you needed to be fairly close to the shed so the caller up could reach you when you had an early turn.

My own holiday was to start on Wednesday 6th September but not before I had another 2P, Saltley's number 40511 on a job with Harry to Up Sidings, another early start at 3-40am.

After my holiday it was back to it with jobs north and also three to Gloucester. Two of the engines are rated VG in my diary and they were 4F's numbers 43891 and 44266. I also had two 8f's but didn't give them a rating at all. This was probably because they were normally a good engine they steamed well and were very strong.

I started October on the passengers again, this time with Ted Love. I managed three days before being off with the flu. From Worcester we had compounds down, 41012 or 41028 Bristol, Barrow Road engines and a Black Five back, 4811 or 4917. I couldn't have been that bad as I was on the bank the following Monday for six days with Dennis Lott doing five trips each day.

After being in No2 Link for a while I was then promoted back to number one and was with Ernie Yeates for a week or two with a mixture of engines including one Crab, 2790. Ernie's nickname was Blossom, possibly because of his love of flowers or maybe because his face was often very red. I think Ernie was from Worcester and probably started at the old Midland shed there. He lived not far from me and went to work on his bike.

I was soon back down to number two link at the beginning of November and worked to Landor St with Les Rudge with 3949. We then worked back from Washwood Heath Jct with Garratt 7979. These Midland Garratts were shedded at Toton and would usually be on the heavier trains. I don't remember having any problem with them unlike our one; I was never short of steam. We also worked on 43043 that week. These engines were popular with firemen if you had to dispose as they had rocking grates which made the job a lot easier. Les was known as All England as he was a driver who would go anywhere and on the Sunday we went to Bescot with 44035. Bristol, Bath or Derby was not out of the question with Les.

Six days with not one minute's overtime was not usual but this was because starting on November 13th I was on the compounds working the passenger trains with Ted Love, Les Rudge and Charlie Trigg. I booked on at 2-30pm every day and was finished by 9pm. Ted Love's nickname was Compound and he really knew how to work these engines, you hardly seemed to use any coal.

The following week I started off on the bank with Charlie Pegler. Charlie was from Stroud originally but came to Bromsgrove from Worcester and later went back down south. He was another one who wore a flat cap, I don't know why drivers did this as a grease top cap could be wiped but a flat cap would soon get covered in oil. It was back on the compounds to finish off the month though with Ted Love.

I didn't give any of the compounds a rating but on the Saturday I gave 4371 a VG when I went to Up Sidings with George Allen. George had the nickname of Blowy as he was a little overweight and would get out of breath. He lived in Millfields next door to another of our drivers Ernie Yeates.

There was no work for me on Christmas Day or Boxing Day but on the 27th I was on the Big-un with Bill Devereax doing five trips on the 8-05am shift.

My birthday was on the 31st and being 21 I went on to top money 117/- per week.

1951

I started the year in No1 Link and on 23rd January was booking on at 7-58am to work an express to Worcester with Bill Bozward, Bill lived in Carlyle Road and was the only driver that I remember that took snuff, he would wash his hankie out in the bucket and the water would turn red.

He would also put his bottle of tea on the regulator quadrant but it was always stewed. We had Saltley loco 2826; I liked these Crabs, they were good engines and were used on passenger and freight. The next three days I was with George Dyer working a return trip to Gloucester. For this job we had Black Fives 4520 and 4545 and Jubilees 5696 Arethusa, 5667 Jellico and 5610 Gold Coast. The Black Fives were Saltley engines but the Jubilees were all from 17A Derby.

Booking on at 7-58am we walked over to the station before getting the 8-18am passenger train to New Street. We relieved a set of men here before working the express to Gloucester where we were relieved. There was a nice big canteen at Gloucester and I think we used to go over there for a bite to eat before walking to Barnwood sidings for our return working, which was a freight job. Arriving at Bromsgrove we would be relieved by a set of our own men. What I remember about working on this express job was the rocking and rolling of the engine, even though I had worked on the compounds I wasn't used to going at these speeds and until I got used to it some of the coal ended up on the footplate and not the fire.

I was on passenger work the following week as well with Charlie Trigg, compounds one way and Black Fives the other. The first day was foggy but I had an experienced driver in Charlie who could tell exactly where we were by the sounds as we went under and over bridges and through cuttings as well as the speed of the train giving a clue as to whether we were on a rising or falling gradient. Later in my career when I was a driver I hated it in the fog and was never as confident as Charlie.

Number 1 Link

11-42pm	8-54pm	2-32am
9-50am	5-58am	7-30am
2-00pm Stoke	10-23pm	9-30pm
4-20am	7-58am Express	Rest Day relief

I was put back down to No2 Link at the beginning of February and nothing much out of the ordinary happened for the next few weeks although I did have a Saltley driver with me on the bank one day by the name of Bates and a job on Super D 8906 to Water Orton with George Stanley. I also had engine 44422 a couple of times, this engine was from Bath Green Park and is unusual in being a left hand drive engine and is still around today. On the 23rd I had Garratt 7996 to Cheltenham with George Stanley, back passenger and no overtime.

I had a week on the bank with George Stanley before being put back up into No 1 Link with Jack Bishop as my regular mate.

On 29th May I had 43027 (21A) and 43048 (17A) on a job to Water Orton and back. Although Saltley had a few of these engines we didn't get to work on them too often as they were mainly on passenger work often down the Redditch branch. Jack Bishop was my mate and we made a few hours overtime.

At the beginning of June I had four days on passenger work with Jack Bishop. On the first day we had what was my first Standard engine 73000 which had only been built in April and Black Five 45088 back. It was two Fives on the Wednesday before 73000 again. These standards were different to what I was used to but I soon got used to them and found them to be good engines and with a rocking grate it made life easier at disposal time. On the Friday it was a five down and only 4F 44201 back.

Towards the end of the month I was on the shed with Harvey Haylings, I didn't seem to get to work with Harvey very often, this was a Sunday job.

The 2nd June was the day I got to work on my first Baby Scot when I went to Landor St with Jack Bishop and loco 45501 St Dunstan's. I think this was the first time I had worked on one of these but there are no comments in my diary so I must have got on alright. This week was spiv week when we booked on at various times to cover people who were having a rest (or Spiv) day.

I had 2 weeks away on holiday to IOM and Ireland in August. I loved it in Ireland the scenery was beautiful and the people were lovely and friendly.

There was excitement at home in November as we had our first television which cost £94. It seems a lot of money as it was only tiny compared with today's sets, I think it only had a 12 inch screen. On the 26th of the month we had another pay rise, the second of the year. My new rate was 136/- per week.

In December I was with Harry Walker for a couple of days on 58100. If he took a liking to you then you were alright but otherwise Harry was not the easiest person to work with; he had come to Bromsgrove from Redditch and later went back there. He was to return to Bromsgrove many years later and worked at eleven depots in all.

1952

The New Year would have been welcomed in the customary way by all the engines blowing their whistles.

I was still in No 1 Link and nothing much had changed except we had lost the 7-58am Express job and the time of the pick-up had changed to 4-13am.

My regular mate for the year was George Stanley although I worked with many others as well. I enjoyed working with George as we shared an interest in music and would have plenty to talk about. In his younger days George had been the conductor of the Walsall Symphony Orchestra and his wife played the piano at the cinema in Bromsgrove.

I had a full week on the Bank with Harry Walker in January but apart from that I only had another five shifts including two on 58100. One of those shifts was with Jim Kirkham who I have not mentioned so far. What I remember about Jim was he wore a flat cap not the usual grease top one and being a heavy smoker his fingers were badly stained with nicotine. It's funny the things that you remember.

The King, George VI died on February 6th, I was with Danny Stainton and 43837 booking on at 2-38pm for a job to Cheltenham. The BBC closed down for the day apart from news bulletins and cinemas and theatres were closed and sporting events cancelled. He was buried the following week.

I was with Reg Probert, known as Pommie, on 22nd March but we only got as far as Brickyard on 4201 before getting relieved. This was not the best area of Birmingham and if you stood around too long children would uncouple some of your wagons. A train was run regularly around here to clear all the rubbish that had been dumped on the railway.

Six days later Ron Stokes was my mate on 44227, with a 3am start we made it as far as Camp Hill. I remember Ron had ginger hair and lived on

Charford. I didn't know Ron very well but I remember he always had plenty to say so it wouldn't have been a boring trip.

On the pick-up in April we only went as far as Spetchley on the Monday. The following three days instead of going on Bromsgrove shed, like we used to, we took the engine to Saltley on two days and to Bournville on the other. This meant that we made a bit of overtime. We always used to have one of our own engines on this job such as 43186 or 43667, but it seemed to have changed to Saltley or Bournville engines.

Booking on at 10-23pm one week in April with George Stanley I was mainly working fitted trains to Landor Street but on April 17 we took 45679 light engine to Gloucester first before working with 42789 to Landor Street. This was the first Jubilee I had been on since working the passengers the year before.

On 12th May I should have been on the Night Goods but was booking on at 12-30pm with Bob Gill and after shunting with either 43186 or 43667 we went to Gloucester. On the Thursday we went as far as Over Sidings which was past Central station on the line to Newport and as my mate didn't sign there we had a pilot man.

A diary entry for Wednesday 28th May reveals my interest in horse racing as it says Tulyar won the Derby at 11-2. It doesn't say whether I backed it.

I exchanged turns for a week in June and was with Harvey Haylings working to Washwood Heath but also included was a trip to Burton (Leicester Jct) with 43917 and Gloucester with 43992. My normal shift would have been 4-20am which was not my favourite time and by swapping I was starting at a more respectable time, these varied between 7am and 10am that week.

For three days in July I was with Joe Ashfield. Joe was only a little chap with dark curly hair, a few years older than me and was a passed fireman. We went to Up Sidings and returned to Bromsgrove with 43926, Landor St with 44841 then Bournville loco with 43847 and Gloucester with 44272 and return to Bromsgrove with 43443.

My annual leave this year was in August and I had two weeks in Jersey.

A week with Jim Core in September included a trip to Burton with 8F 48341. This was a long day as we booked on at 2-38pm and didn't finish until 4-25am the next day and we only worked the one way. We had to have twelve hours rest and so we didn't book on the next day until 4-35pm and a job to Landor St.

I have mentioned Jack Bishop a few times but there was also another Bishop who was a driver, Ben, although not related. I was with Ben for a few days in October. A thing that I remember about Ben was the way he brought his tea to work. Some men would bring some tea in a bottle or tea and sugar in a small jar and some milk in a bottle but he brought his tea, sugar and condensed milk all wrapped up in a twist of newspaper. This was a right sticky mess. I also remember Ben would often cause arguments when we had union meetings. Some of these meetings could get quite heated and it was even known for fights to break out.

In October the Night Goods had returned to normal with our own engine. I was with George Stanley and 43667 for five days making it to Up Sidings on three days and only as far as Hazlewell on the other two. Passing Barnt Green on a night job such as this I was always fascinated by the way the embankment was lit up by glow-worms, I wonder if there are still some there.

Towards the end of the year a little Pug number 56020 arrived on shed this had been sent to us to heat the oil for the Garratt which was due to return as an oil fired engine. Some refuelling equipment had also been installed at the shed next to number three road, it looked a bit like a water column. As they were having problems with the Garrett at Gorton the Pug and refueler lay unused for some years.

My pay went up by 7/- in November to 143/- per week.

Fire Cleaning

On the bankers fire cleaning was carried out as required, usually on the ash pit. When you started your shift you would be told how many trips were in the fire so you would have an idea when it would need cleaning. A Jinty was quite straightforward as the firebox was not very big. Using the clinker shovel all the good fire at the back of the box was moved to the front with the clinker shovel then with the bent fire iron the clinker would be lifted from the firebars and shovelled out with the clinker shovel. The good fire was then moved back under the door with the shovel and the clinker removed from the front bars with the straight dart and shovelled out. With all the clinker removed the fire was spread around the box and fresh coal put on to build the fire back up. The smokebox and ashpan would also have to be emptied. When your allowed time was up you had to be prepared with a good fire and plenty of steam ready to bank again. On days the lamps would all have to be trimmed and filled as well. Returning to the coal stage water would be taken and the bunker replenished.

Fire Cleaning on 2290/58100

With a lot bigger grate it was a much harder task to clean the fire on the Big-un. Because the box was so long and we hadn't got a clinker shovel long enough we had to do it a bit differently. First we would shovel the good fire from the back of the box to the front, and then all the clinker would be got off the bars with the dart and using the fire that had been moved to the front to push against shovel it all out. Then with what we called the long rake all the fire would be pulled up under the door with the clinker loosened at the front it would be pulled back over the good fire and removed with the clinker shovel.

The shovel would get very hot and get out of shape and would have to be straightened out with a hammer. The ashpan would also be raked out and to keep the dust down there was a hosepipe in the pit which you could set to make the job as comfortable as possible although the dust still seemed to get everywhere. The smokebox would be emptied and when Eric Underhill was a cleaner in the mid-fifties he remembers being sent down to the South where a steam lance was kept by the ashpit. This would be connected up and he would proceed to blow the tubes out as I had done years earlier at the shed and like me he would get a blowback and a black face.

1953

My new mate for the year was Bill Phelps, known as Frisky Bill, with most of the work being on the main line, I didn't get to do any banking until Easter Monday. Bill and I booked on at 6-05am and did two trips with 47313, it was probably a Sunday service and no freights either.

No 1 Link

9-30pm Night Goods	2-00pm Stoke (Salto)	10-23pm
Rest Day Relief	4-20am	2-32am
11-42pm	10-15pm	2-38pm
9-49am	4-16am Pick-up	7-30am

On 15th of January Bill and I worked 43847 to Cheltenham and my diary then says we had 58100 but gives no other details. Perhaps it had been to Gloucester for repair and was returning home. Charlie Berwick remembers taking her there on a couple of occasions.

We still seemed to be using Bournville engines a lot on the 4-16am Ashchurch pick-up and we returned the engine there four times when on the job in February. One of the benefits of this job that I haven't mentioned is if you had a word with the platelayer he would leave you a rabbit or two round the back of his hut the next day in exchange for half a crown. I never did this myself as at home, like most of our neighbours, we had about a dozen Flemish Giant rabbits which had plenty of meat on them and I can remember having rabbit for Christmas lunch. Meat rationing was still in force at this time.

Bournville shed was a roundhouse and after disposing of the engine we would leave the engine inside the shed. I remember the coaling facilities there. You would have to wheel the tubs of coal and tip them into the tender. This was not very modern but better than we had at Bromsgrove.

I had been having trouble with my ears for some time and was now having penicillin injections, this seemed to have cleared up by the time I had my fortnights leave at the end of April and beginning of May.

I had a long weekend at the end of May as I was booked off on the 31st and spiv day on the Monday followed by another day off for the Coronation on the 2nd June.

My next job on the bank was on Sunday 21st June with Charlie Pegler when we booked on at 5-47am and did two trips with 47276. This was an ideal opportunity to cook yourself some breakfast on the shovel especially if you did an early trip. Arriving back at Bromsgrove the fire would be well burnt through and you would have plenty of time before your next trip.

With the injector on it was possible to use the slacking pipe to wash the shovel before wiping it with a clean rag. A lump of fat put on the shovel would soon melt and be hot enough for two or three rashers of bacon to be added, care had to be taken here as it would be cooked in no time and done to a shrivel. The bacon was placed on a couple of thick slices of bread that were waiting and then the egg was cracked into the hot fat, by this time your mouth was watering and your mate, who might only have cheese sandwiches, was wishing he had brought some too. Wiping the yolk from around your mouth it was then off to the cabin to make some tea to wash it down.

I must have been getting interested in tennis by this time as on 3rd July I have noted Vic Seixas, an American, winning the men's single title at Wimbledon and the next day Mo Connolly another American, winning the Women's title.

I was only to work on the bank once more until the end of the year and that was August Bank Holiday Monday with Wilf Panting on 43673, an engine on loan from Saltley, two trips and a 5-00am start.

During the year I had eleven Sunday jobs, two on the bank, one on shed and nine on the main line. Most of these were up the bank to Washwood Heath or Water Orton but also to Cheltenham and Gloucester. These Sunday jobs were very welcome as they boosted your money up a bit.

I had a busy time leading up to Christmas working eleven days in a row and finishing at 8-30pm on Christmas Eve after five trips up the bank with Wilf Vallender and 47425. This period included when I was with Bob Gill on 21st December and after booking on at 12-30pm we travelled to Barnt Green before relieving the men on 44378. I don't remember whether the engine was in bad condition or the fire was clinkered up but I have recorded in my diary that we stuck for steam at Cleeve. We seem to have made it to Cheltenham and then put the train inside and returned to Bromsgrove light engine. We would have left her on the shed before finishing at 11-45pm. This is the only time I have recorded being short of steam on the main line or Down the Nick as we called it.

The next two days I had better luck with Bob and we made it to Gloucester both days with 43928 and 43645.

I didn't usually work my birthday but this year was an exception as I booked on at 7-20am with Jack Jay? and did six trips on 47308.

I don't know whether Worcester had got another fireman but I didn't do any passenger work this year.

I don't remember Sid Taylor but his name appears in my diary in August when I worked with him on nine occasions on 3F's and 4F's to Gloucester, Up Sidings and Landor St.

1954

I started the New Year as I'd finished the last with three days on the bank. The first two with Harry Jay and 47308 starting at 7-20am and doing five trips each day. I don't remember much about Harry but Gordon Russell knew him well as he worked with him at Redditch. His full name was Henry John Jay and he walked with a limp after losing four toes from his left foot. I think he came to us from Redditch and I don't think he was at Bromsgrove very long. On Sunday 3rd I was with Harvey Haylings on 47305 starting at 4-20am and managing three trips.

The No 1 link that I was in was more or less the same as the previous year and most of my work was on the main line with days here and there on the bank including only one day on 58100 with Harold Brassington. I didn't work with Harold a lot; he had come to Bromsgrove from Saltley and later moved back there. My new mate for the year was Jim Core but I also worked with lots of others too.

I was now on the top firing rate of 147/- but this went up on the 24th January to 151/6d and when I was driving to 159/6d. By the end of the year the firing rate had gone up again to 158/6d and my rate for driving to 172/6d.

With Jim on January 8th we had booked on at 10-15pm and were headed for Washwood Heath with 44272 but instead of going the usual way via Camp hill we went through New Street. We still didn't get to Up Sidings very quickly though and we booked off at 9-15am the next day after returning on the cushions.

With Jim Core as my mate I was always going to get a few jobs to Burton and on 5th April we took 47303 there light engine and back passenger. I don't remember now but this was one of our own engines so I expect it was headed for Derby Works.

This was an important year for me as I was due to be passed out as a driver. Ever since I had started on the railway I had been learning about the engines, working of trains and track layouts and signalling not to mention the Rule Book. Apart from in the bank engine siding and on shed I had not had the opportunity to do much driving, Danny Stainton was one of the few who would let you have a go. I think Danny was originally from Crewe, very pleasant to work with, he usually had a fag hanging from the corner of his mouth and his eyes always seemed to be watering.

I had been swatting very hard in the last few months and Inspector Bates or Wood had visited and helped me prepare for the big day. Tuesday January 26th was the day and I was very nervous when I booked on at 8-00am. Mr Bates arrived and asked me loads of questions on the Rule Book which I knew almost off by heart by now so I had no problems there. Next it was the engine test with loads of questions about the workings of a steam engine. It was possible to choose which motion you answered questions on and I had chosen the Stephenson Link Motion not Walschaerts. I probably did this as the Jinties and all the 3 and 4f's I worked on had this type of motion. I must have done my homework correctly as Mr Bates informed me that I had passed. It was now down to the practical. For this we travelled passenger to New Street from where I drove a passenger train back to Bromsgrove with 43013. Arriving at Bromsgrove I was told that subject to a medical I was now a Passed Fireman. I booked off at 4-00pm and was over the moon and probably cycled home in record time to tell my parents.

Exam Questions

Although I don't remember the exact questions that I was asked you needed to know the answers to them all. Here is a selection from The Handbook for Railway Steam Locomotive Enginemen.

Q. What action would you take in the event of a melted fusible plug?

Q. What purpose is served by the continuous blowdown valve?

Q. What is priming and foaming? What would you do when either occurs?

Q. Explain the working principles of a movable combining-cone type of injector.

Q. If one of the top feed clacks sticks up when working a train, what steps would you take?

Q. What are the eight named positions of the crank?

Q. Describe in detail a typical steam cycle in the front end of the cylinder during one revolution of the driving wheels, the gear being in a position giving about 30% cut-off.

Q. Describe the Stephenson's link motion.

Q. Explain briefly the working of this valve gear.

Q. In the case of a broken or bent side rod, what should be done?

Q. Why is the cylinder oil issued for the piston and valves of non-superheated engine different from that issued for superheated engines?

Q. Describe the brake action on a train fitted throughout with the vacuum automatic brake.

Q. Name a few bad faults to be avoided when handling vacuum fitted trains.

As you can see there is a lot to be learnt if you wanted to be a driver and you needed to do a lot of studying to be able to get through. If you want to know the answers I think you may still be able to get a copy of this book or one similar.

It was an 8-00am start the next day as I had to travel to Swindon for my medical which I passed and a 4-00pm finish. I would also have to sign my road cards, to the north I signed as far as Water Orton, via Camp Hill and New St and Gloucester in the south via the Old Road and Worcester.

I should have been on at 2-32am this week with my mate Jim Core but because of my drivers tests I was with Bill Phelps the next day starting at 5-00am and firing to Landor St with 43484.

Mr Bates had not finished with me however and he was at Bromsgrove again on the Friday for my first driving turn. It was an 8-00am start and my first job was to prepare 43186.

At 12-15pm the 10-05am Worcester to Washwood Heath arrived at Bromsgrove and I relieved the driver and along with a Worcester fireman we left at 12-20pm with 50 empties and 9 goods. The loco was 44660 and I would think we had two bankers. We passed Blackwell at 12-35pm and Barnt Green four minutes later. Kings Norton was passed at 12-49pm before arriving at Camp Hill at 12-59pm. After being relieved at 1-05pm by Bromsgrove men we made our way to Bournville station and waited for the 2-00pm Birmingham to Worcester passenger. The train, headed by 43013, arrived at Bournville at 2-18pm and we relieved the crew and set off at 2-20pm with three coaches.

We stopped at Kings Norton for two minutes 2-24pm to 2-26pm, Northfield 2-31pm to 2-32pm, Barnt Green 2-32pm to 2-34pm which I recorded as two minutes late, Blackwell 2-38pm to 2-40pm arriving at Bromsgrove at 2-45pm where we were relieved by Worcester men. It was not easy working these passenger jobs as the vacuum brake took some getting used to and you had to stop in the correct place on the platform, if you panicked and put too much brake in you would stop short. I booked off at the shed at 3-05pm and that was my first driving turn over.

Twelve hours later I booked on with my own mate Jim Core and worked to Gloucester on 43464 and then travelled back passenger.

I finished off the week with a Sunday job, a 1-28am start to work a freight with 42872 to Gloucester and 43507 back with another goods, George Stanley being my mate and a 9-30am finish.

I had to wait a few weeks for my next driving turn which would be the first without an inspector with me. This came on 11th April and was a Sunday ballast job. My mate was Norman Rudge and we booked on at 11-45am. With loco 43680 we left Bromsgrove at 12-05pm with 10 wagons equal to 17 mineral and headed to Droitwich. After half an hour there we went back north to Halesowen Jct where we spent nearly two hours. Leaving there at 3-25pm we went back to Droitwich before running round and returning to Bromsgrove and disposing of the engine and finishing at 5-45pm.

My next driving job was on a Sunday again but this time on 4-05pm bank with Royston Cummings as my mate and loco 47313. We did just two trips and finished at 12-35am.

It was two months before my next driving turn on 4th July. For T93 I booked on at 4-39am with Sid Usher as my mate. After a long wait in the cabin our train of 26 empties arrived from Cheltenham hauled by 43828. After taking water we left Bromsgrove at 7-30am and worked to Washwood Heath. From here we went light engine to Saltley and got a lift home in the brake van of a freight train. We eventually booked off at 1-55pm. It was shed duties next on 15th August when with Joe Ashfield and an 8-00am start we disposed of seven engines and prepared one. The engines in question were 47425, 47303, 47313, 47565, 43462, 43186 and 47301. This is the last time I recorded working with Joe and he later left for Old Oak Common probably to get his driving job.

My first trip south as a driver was another Sunday job on 24th October when along with Phillip Rudge I worked the 7-00am from Kings Norton to Gloucester. Phillip was another sporting railwayman as he was a fast bowler for Garringtons. I had worked this job just two weeks before as a fireman with George Stanley and the same engine so knew the routine. We left Bromsgrove with 43462 at 6-30am light engine to Kings Norton where we arrived at 7-00am. We left at 7-50am with 36=40 mineral and arrived at Gloucester at 2-15pm. This was with a 30 minute stop at Bromsgrove to pick up the brakes and take water and ten minutes for signals at Abbotswood. We travelled back home on an express, it was possible to do that in those days of course as they all stopped at Bromsgrove for a banker. I had other driving jobs before the end of the year on the bank, shed and main line with Tony Corcoran, Lawrence Kendal and Bob Gisborne giving me a total of 13.

For three of these jobs, although counting as driving turns, I was actually firing. This was because although I was entitled to the driving job and got paid driving rate we were short of fireman and I had to fire for a driver who was working his rest day.

Although I didn't get to work on the passengers with compounds this year I did have one on 21st June, my first day back after two weeks in Jersey, when after working a freight to Up Sidings with Jim Kirkham and 43846 we took 41195 back light engine to Bromsgrove. Another class of engine that was unusual was class 5 2-6-0 42846 which I fired to Exchange Sidings with Jim Core on 8th December. Exchange Sidings were near Grand Junction signalbox where there was a junction between the Midland and LNWR lines; we didn't go there very often.

I did quite well over the year for Sunday jobs with twenty one in total. Four on the bank, two on shed duties, two on ballast and thirteen on the main line.

1955

Looking through my diary for this year it is not clear who my booked mate was as I seemed to work with everyone at some time or other after starting off with Doug Miller for a few weeks. By the end of the year I was with Fred Bourne for the last couple of months and of course I had 40 driving turns during the year as well. Two of these driving turns were unusual as I was conducting my own mate Jack Richardson from Cheltenham to Gloucester on 17th February with 44299 and 30 loaded wagons, this gave me 25 minutes driving money. From Gloucester we returned home on the cushions. After going north the next day I had what was my 21st driving turn on the Saturday when I conducted Jack again from Cheltenham to Gloucester with 42 mineral and 44026 and back to Cheltenham light engine with Compound 40116 which we continued to Bromsgrove with. This was an easy enough job but having booked on at 10-59pm we didn't finish until 8-30am on the Sunday morning so it was very profitable.

Just when we thought the winter was coming to an end we had a big fall of snow the following week when I had a few days on the bank with Harry Marsh. I seemed to have lots of colds and flu and I had been off for a few days in January and now in March my diary says I have a nasty cold and cough though still at work

I think I have already said how long it could take to get to Birmingham at times and Tuesday 1st March was a good example. I had booked on at 3-45pm Control Relief with Gordon Loat as my fireman and we relieved the 11-45 Westerleigh to Branston at Bromsgrove with 44332. We left Bromsgrove at 5-25pm with 50 empties and arrived at Kings Norton at 6-15pm and this is where we stayed until our signal came off at 12-10am eventually arriving at Landor St at 1-25am and finally booking off at 5-10am. This stretch of line was known as The Golden Mile as so much overtime was made here. There was pub nearby The Camp I think it was called and many men made use of this and drank their overtime away.

In May we had a general election which the Tories won by 62 seats and a few days later ASLEF called its members out on strike. I was in the NUR so worked as normal though there were obviously a lot less trains running. The men at Bromsgrove were split about 50/50 ASLEF and NUR and the strikers were picketing at the South and at the shed. On 14th June I was with George Dyer working on 43462 to Up Sidings and back to Bromsgrove when we heard the strike had been called off just after 6-00pm. The strike had lasted for seventeen days and resulted in the drivers getting a rise but not firemen. This strike caused a lot of bad feeling and some men would not speak to each other for a long time after.

My holiday this year was in July and was spent in Ostend where I remember having the best fish and chips ever.

The 1st of August was a Bank holiday and I went to Chepstow races before returning to work on the bank with Jim Roberts for five days.

We had been expecting the Garratt back for a long time and it finally arrived in July fitted for oil firing so we thought perhaps it would be a lot easier to work on now.

* * * * *

The first test for 69999 was on Tuesday 9th August. I was with Bob Gill having booked on at 8-30am and disposing of 58100 we took the Garratt down to the south. By mid-day we were standing first at the coal stage and at 12-10pm a heavy china clay train came up requiring two bankers and so we buffered up behind it. I had no training on oil firing but there was an inspector on the footplate who told me what to do. Despite following instructions we still were not making much steam by the time we set off. The situation didn't improve and before we got too far up the bank it was obvious we were not going to make it and so we came to a stand. After a wait for a couple more engines to arrive we got under way and made it to Blackwell. After returning to Bromsgrove we went to shed and that was the end of the trial for the day.

I'm not sure how many days the Garratt worked but Eric Underhill remembers doing one shift on it with Vic Randall and accompanied by an inspector. There were a lot of valves for adjusting the oil flow and the inspector gave Eric instructions on which ones to turn. Although not blowing off they had a fair amount of steam to start with but as they went up the bank it began to drop back and the top of the bank couldn't come soon enough. To return to Bromsgrove they had to have the road through the station as the brake was very poor and they probably wouldn't have been able to stop.

Also in August a 9F number 92008 arrived at Bromsgrove for a trial and this was more successful. I didn't get to work on it but Eric Underhill remembers an incident when he was working on it. I think it was with us for a couple of weeks. This is what Eric remembers:

> *On nights when banking a train with a tankie in front we had a terrific wheel spin and came to a stand. The train with only one banker now also came to a stand a bit further up the bank. We couldn't close the regulator and all the fire was being drawn out of the firebox and up the chimney. My mate was Albert Jakeman. The driver on the tankie, Ben Bishop, and his mate jumped off their engine as they thought if the 9f found its feet it would run into them. We eventually got the regulator closed but not before the track was badly damaged. There was an enquiry and it was found there was a fault with the regulators and they were modified. My mate that night, Albert, was well known for his homemade parsnip wine which he sometimes brought to work, it was very moreish but also very deadly.*

Apart from this incident the trial was successful and cleaning the fire was a lot easier than on 58100 as it had a rocking grate so if the Big-un was soon to be withdrawn as had been rumoured these engines would seem to be an ideal replacement.

I seemed to work a lot more on the bank this year with 59 turns, 20 of which were driving, including 4 on 58100.

The Garratt didn't stay long at Bromsgrove and with the Lancashire and Yorkshire Pug 51217 no longer required it was sent to Derby. One September Sunday morning Sid Usher booked on with his driver George Dyer to take the engine away. Ben Bishop was foreman at the time and Sid remembers George patting the tank and saying to Ben "she isn't very warm yet Ben". Ben replied "she's been lit up for some time George". With the coal stacked each side of the footplate and the tank full they set off with a banker to help conserve some coal and water. The water levelling pipe between the two sides of the tank was blocked and so they didn't have the use of the whole tank. Sid thinks that Bournville shed was probably their first stop for coal and water but can't remember for sure. They then carried on to Camp Hill where they made another stop for water and they then topped up again at Landor St. Whenever they stopped they looked around for coal and threw it up on the engine and begged for some from signalmen too. At Bromford they were put inside and then were put on the slow line at Water Orton. Top speed was only about 10mph and so they were put in the loop at Perrin and Harrison Sidings just north of Wilmcote for a blow up, the signalman here let them have some of his coal. More water was taken at Whitacre and Sid reckons they are the only ones ever to take coal on Tamworth troughs; it was probably what was washed off tenders. More water was taken here too and then at Wichnor. Next stop was Burton shed where they called for coal and water before continuing on their way. Another stop was made at Clay Mills for water and Sid remembers sitting on the fence there, the first sit down he'd had since leaving Bromsgrove. The end of the journey was in sight now but there was single line working at Repton and Willington so they welcomed a pilotman aboard he looked a bit surprised when he saw the engine and said "I've never been on one of these engines before". Eventually Derby shed was reached, just as well as there was no coal or water left. Having already got their day in they didn't have to dispose of the engine and it was left on the ash pit. It must have been heaven returning home on the cushions after that mammoth journey. Back in Birmingham Sid remembers the Battle of Britain celebrations were taking place so this was probably mid-September.

They must have thought Sid did a good job taking the Pug to Derby as he had another job on one on a Monday morning, this time with Tom Newman. It may have been the same engine as it was later transferred to Bristol. The engine had been brought to Bromsgrove the previous day by Bromsgrove men, John Rudge was the fireman but Sid can't recollect who the driver was. Tom and Sid were supposed to go as far as Gloucester but they were holding trains up as they had to stop at Dunhampstead for a blow up. They struggled on to Defford and then a following train pushed them to Eckington where they were relieved by Gloucester men the driver being appropriately named Delay. There had been plenty of delays that day.

In September I worked with Tom Field again, the first time since 1947 when I had a week with him on 08-05 bank. I was with him on 08-05 bank again with 47425 before going driving on the Carriage and Wagon with Mike Vallender as my mate.

I was on the bank again with him on the Wednesday and Friday with 47301 but never worked with him again. I think he was once at Saltley so perhaps he went back there. What I do remember about him was that he always wore bicycle clips to stop the dust going up his legs. He lived up Finstall near Vic Randall.

On the main line there were a lot more 8F's about and I worked on 20 during the year.

On Saturday 19th November with Fred Bourne I had my first Standard of the year when we worked to Water Orton and back to West End with 73045. This was the first time I had fired one of these on a freight train.

I liked to have my birthday off but this year, my 12th on the railway, I was on 47303 with Fred Bourne booking on at 7-20am and doing five trips.

1956

I began the year earning 164/- a week when firing and 176/- when driving but we had a rise on the 23rd of the month to 175/6d and 188/6d. My new mate for the year was Charlie Evans and we started off the year by booking on at 3-45pm and working a goods train with an 8F to Duddeston Road. The number of these engines was increasing and by the end of the year I had fired or driven 39, almost twice as many as the year before.

9f's were also being introduced and my first job on one was firing for Doug Miller on 92051 on a job to Burton on the 8th of March. I had another a month later with my own mate to Up Sidings, this was with 92045. 92058 was our engine twice the next month, light engine to Saltley then a freight to Gloucester. Having some experience on these engines was to come in handy in view of what was to happen on the bank with the loss of 58100.

In the first four months of the year I had fired 58100 three times and had two days driving her but on Sunday the 6th May I was on her for the last time with my mate Charlie Evans. I should have been driving her this day but we were short of fireman so although I was paid driving rate I was doing the firing. This was my 80th driving turn and we did three trips on the 8-05 shift.

Taking 58100 to Derby. 7th May 1956

The following is an account by Barry Troth of 58100 leaving Bromsgrove for the last time.

> *58100 worked right to the end of her time at Bromsgrove. Reg Probert and Les Wood were driver and fireman when they banked the mail about 3-30 in the morning. On her return to Bromsgrove they took the engine to shed where they were relieved by Driver Les Rudge and myself. We had booked on at 4-00am and after taking water we left for Derby around 4-30am. Despite Les having a reputation for fast running we never went particularly fast. This was just as well as stopping to take water at Kingsbury we found we had a hot box but after a period of cooling down and some more oil we continued on our way. On arriving at Derby shed at around 8 or 9 o'clock I threw out the fire, cleaned out the ashpan and emptied the smokebox before leaving the engine behind her replacement 92079. This engine was at Derby to have the tender cut out to make coaling easier at Bromsgrove and to receive the headlamp and generator off the Big-un. I noticed that the tender had already been modified so as soon as the lamp and generator were fitted she would be sent south to Bromsgrove. Les and I then returned to Bromsgrove on the cushions. We caught a train to New St and then the 12-15 to Bromsgrove where we booked off around 1-00pm.*

I had some slightly different work the next month when on 11th and 12th of June I was conducting on a Tamping machine. I'm not sure where this was but was probably down the Old Road.

At the end of the week on Saturday 16th I had my first turn on 92079 with Vic Randall. It was a busy day with six trips though thankfully the fire cleaning would have been easier than on 58100. When working with Vic there was no drinking tea from the can lid or from a bottle he would lay a cloth out and produce two nice china cups from his bag before pouring the tea from the can for himself and his mate.

I wasn't to work on her again until October when after having 92103 on a job to Landor St with Charlie on Monday 1st I had a driving turn on her on 12-05am with Derek Harris on the Friday managing four trips for my 150th driving turn. The cab on the standards was completely different to the Midland engines that we were used to and the driving position was on the left. There was a comfortable seat for both driver and fireman and the driver could see the signals himself and didn't have to rely on his fireman. The regulator pulled out towards you instead of up as was usual but we still had the headlamp off 58100 to aid us in the dark. Although it was sad to see the Big-un go and the replacement was not unique to the Lickey I think we all got to like her. With 250lbs steam pressure instead of 180 she was very powerful even with two cylinders and not four. The driving wheels were bigger at five foot compared to four foot seven and a half and there was no flange on the centre pair of driving wheels but it was heavier with more weight on each axle. For the fireman the firebox was bigger and the injector controls handily placed on his side of the footplate.

By this time Super D's were not so common but on 18th July I had 47994 from Landor St to Washford Heath after working up from Bromsgrove with 48627.

The first Monday in August was a bank holiday at one time and on the 6th I was on stand-by at the shed with Charlie. We booked on at 8-00am but there was obviously no need for us and we booked off at 10-50am. It may have spoilt our weekend but we got a day in lieu which we could use later.

The previous week I had been driving every day, once to Gloucester with 48103 and a Saltley fireman, this was turn 101 booking on at 9-57pm (8-45pm on the Saturday) and up to Birmingham the rest of the week. With another Saltley fireman on the Thursday and Mike Carter and Gordon Griffiths on the other days we worked fitted trains a lot faster than the normal mineral which I described earlier. On Friday 3rd Gordon Griffiths and I left Bromsgrove with 44378 and 41=43 at 10-47pm, passed Kings Norton at 11-10pm, Kings Heath 11-20pm before arriving at Landor St at 11-30pm where we were relieved. Following this we worked 38 mineral to Washwood Heath Up Sidings with 44263 before taking the loco to Saltley and disposing. We were back at Bromsgrove and booked off in less than eight hours.

We had a new arrival at Bromsgrove during the summer when a Western pannier tank number 8402 arrived and I had my first turn on it driving on 8th August with Saltley fireman Dodds. We did five trips that day. We soon got used to this Western engine and found it more powerful than the Jinties and it would steam well without the need of a jimmy. The big western shovel was not to our liking though and was soon changed for a smaller Midland one. One other thing that was not liked was the water controls for the injectors which were right down in the corner on the fireman's side but we soon got used to this.

On 2nd October, 12-05am with John Gilder as my mate I failed 47638 with a fusible plug leaking badly and exchanged it for 43762. We banked three trains and the last of these was a goods train that took 31 minutes to get to Blackwell. I was informed by the guard that he should have had two bankers but we were possibly the only one available and we caused the 7-43am passenger train to be stopped.

I had a couple of days firing 8402 at the end of October with Joe Clapton before driving again on 2nd November with Stuart Pinfield as my fireman for five trips. In the next few weeks some more of these engines were transferred to Bromsgrove until we had 8400-06 and some of the Jinties were transferred away.

On the 29th December when on shed duties with Ernie Bluck disposing 3186 preparing 3762 and disposing and preparing 8403 and 8400 the latter engine became derailed. This wasn't too unusual and with the aid of some packing the fitters would have soon had us back on.

A footplate ride up the Bank

We used to get a lot of visitors down at the South many of them requesting a cab ride, some of these visits were official but most of them not. I remember people from Australia and New Zealand coming with us on the footplate.

The New Zealanders were dental surgeons and were very keen to fire the engine so they rolled their sleeves up and got stuck in. Not all drivers would welcome people on to the footplate even though there was a chance of some money or a packet of cigarettes being thrust in your hand but I gave many rides even though it was against the rules. Sundays were probably the best days for this so if you haven't already been up the bank with me perhaps you would like to take a trip now.

58100 would probably be your choice of engine so let's go back to Sunday 8th April 1956. Your timing is good as there has been talk in the cabin that the Big-un is nearing the end of its days and may not return from Derby after its next visit. Turn 19 is the 8-05am bank job on 58100 and I had booked on with my mate Brian Perkins, this was my 72nd driving turn.

As you step from the coal stage onto our engine you will be struck by the smell of steam and oil and the sound of sizzling as water dripped from a minor leak onto the drip tray. You will also notice the heat from the fire even though my mate has not got it hot yet. My diary doesn't record the state of the fire but let us assume we have lumped it as there are a number of extra freights due up today and we are expecting to be busy. To lump the fire I would have helped my mate throw as many big lumps in as we could get.

As you sit down on the fireman's seat an express runs by on the mainline and with the steam brake on Brian releases the handbrake and then opens the dampers as I put her in full forward gear. A shout from my mate tells me the dummy is off and with the steam brake off a tug on the regulator gets us going out of the bank engine siding and towards the rear of the train. As we do so I close the cylinder drain cocks, firstly because they don't need to be open now we are under way but also to aid visibility. If it was dark my mate would have switched the headlamp on by turning the steam valve to start the generator. As we buffer up to the rear of the train and wait for the train engine to reply to our whistle you have time to look over my side of the engine to the extensive Carriage and Wagon sidings and a number of huts belonging to brakesmen and wheel tappers and on the other side to the coal sidings and goods shed built in 1898.

After hearing the crow (cock a doodle doo) from the train engine I open the regulator and we get underway, not too much power straight away as it was still possible to slip even with ten driving wheels, it is such a powerful engine. This is what we called losing her feet or dancing. As we increased speed I notched her back by about 15% and opened the regulator some more. A glance at my watch shows it is 9-23 and I make a note in my book.

We are soon thundering past the station box and into the platform with the regulator wide open. Looking to the right you will see the engine shed and all the wagon works buildings beyond. The sound bounces back from the platform buildings and the wall where there was once a bookstall before we pass the water column at the end of the platform and pass under St Godwalds Bridge and get onto the bank. Up through the cutting and speed settles down as we pass the up starter signal.

The blast from the chimney has livened the fire up nicely now and we have plenty of steam as we pass under the Finstall Road bridge and the old chapel and graveyard on the right. As we leave the cutting for an embankment there are some bungalows on the right and fields on the left where there used to be a lot of rabbits before myxomatosis struck. My mate had been looking out and gave me the nod that the automatics were off and we continued through open country with Caspidge Farm on the right. We then blast past Pikes Pool and pass over the catch points and past a small reservoir on the right which feeds the water columns at Bromsgrove and on we pound towards Vigo. This is a popular place for enthusiasts and there are a number there already this morning. As we head towards the distant signal for Blackwell my mate puts both injectors on as the water level was now dropping and we needed it to be towards the top of the glass when we levelled out at the summit.

On the left is the Convalescent Home a well-known landmark and on the right there is a line of Poplar trees that sometimes cause us a problem in the autumn but not today and we enter the cutting for the final part of the bank. Past some more catch points and the Blackwell home signal and we are through the station and with no indication from the signalman that we are to cross by the box I give a good push on past the goods yard on the left. With the blower on I close the regulator and the train pulls away and it is time to brake.

As we come to a stand both dummies come off and we go straight through the bankers siding and wait at the starter. While we are waiting I take the opportunity to note down the time we got to Blackwell, 9-31. We don't have long to wait and after getting under way I make a note in my book of the time, 9-34. We return at a steady speed down the bank using the steam brake and arriving back at Bromsgrove at 9-45. If we had some tankies behind us on our return my mate would have wound the tender handbrake on and the rear engine would have a bit of steam on to keep us together. Unusually there were two handbrakes on the Big-un, the other being on the engine. This was the first of five trips that day, one more passenger and then three goods.

1957

I started off the year on the bank with George Pidgeon and 92079 but on Thursday 3rd January I had a driving turn with Ken Suckling to Landor St with 42896 and then down to Stoke Works with our own engine 43186. On the Saturday I was driving again on 92079 with Michael Metcalf as my mate. We did five trips on the 4-05pm shift and one of them must have been late on as we didn't book off until 1-20am on the Sunday morning.

The next week with Joe Clapton we nearly had a full house when we worked on five of the six panniers that were now allocated to us. Only 8403 evaded us, on the other day we had Jinty 47308.

After the 15th I was with my new mate Bill Phelps doing main line and bank work.

On 30th January Bill and I had a different destination when we worked 92101 on a freight to Castle Bromwich Bay, something that we repeated later in the year. I don't think there was a bay platform at Castle Bromwich but I think this may have been the goods road at the back of the platform where we were relieved.

I probably had to fill out a report on the 18th February when I was driving 48523 light engine to Bournville shed with Goodwin Layton as my mate. The loco had had a new axlebox and was running in so we couldn't go too fast and we stopped an express. Having booked on at 5-00am we left Bromsgrove at 9-45 and arrived at Bournville at 11-20.

Even after the arrival of the panniers the Jinties were still often used on bank work and in April I had three driving turns on 7308, 7313 and 7638 with mates Barry Troth, Trevor Annetts and Alan Janssen.

My holidays were earlier this year and on the 12th May I set off for San Remo in Italy with my Uncle Jack.

Most railwaymen spent their holidays in this country and so liked to have the summer weeks and that was probably why I had four weeks

Up express running past the South Box 16-4-55. The box has still got its original roof here but it was replaced by a flat roof after a fire early one morning. The signalman, Basil Glover, was said to have put a detonator on the fire to clear the chimney. I think this was in the early sixties. R S Carpenter Photos.

58100 descending the bank at Blackwell 16-4-55. Author's collection.

Double headed up freight in the cutting at Blackwell. Author's collection.

On another occasion when our regular engine was away, 92155 drops off an express at Blackwell in 1963. 92157 is in the loop. P A Bridgman. Author's collection.

43186 taking water on the up goods while waiting to attack the bank 10-4-52. Roger Carpenter Photo.

A later picture of the Salto taken on August 3rd 1964 showing 8403 between the bridges at the bottom of the bank. Norman Fox.

42823 at Barnt Green on a local passenger in late 50s. R S Carpenter Photos.

5226 on shed in 1959 Author's collection.

The shed as it was on 5th July 1959. Roger Carpenter collection.

43762 approaching Vigo with the Salto in 1959. Author's collection.

Double headed express at Pikes Pool 15-2-60. R J Sellick.

92079 at Bromsgrove 5-8-61. She has now lost her headlamp. Copyright T J Edgington.

BRITISH RAILWAYS	STORES DEMAND NOTE	No.		B.R. 8752

R & M Dept. Shop or Station Bromsgrove Date 18·10·61

Description: Fire Bars

Charge to: 8487

Catalogue No. 42-138 QTY. 5

Stores Issue Stamp

Only one item must be entered on this Demand Note

Foreman's Signature: A Core

BRITISH RAILWAYS	STORES DEMAND NOTE	No.		B.R. 8752

R & M Dept. Shop or Station Bromsgrove Date 19/10/61

Description: Lead Plugs 26's

Charge to: 9430

Catalogue No. 25/47770 QTY. 2

Stores Issue Stamp

Only one item must be entered on this Demand Note

Foreman's Signature: A Core

BRITISH RAILWAYS	STORES DEMAND NOTE	No.		B.R. 8752

Dept. Shop or Station Bromsgrove Date 12·10·61

Description: Mud hole Joint

Charge to: 47276

Catalogue No. 2/670 QTY. 1

Stores Issue Stamp

Only one item must be entered on this Demand Note

Foreman's Signature: A Core

Stores Demand Notes from 1961 showing the sort of things that were kept in the stores. All signed by the Shedmaster Jim Core.

8401 with driver Charlie Evans and 8403 with Bert Halfpenny assist a passenger at Pikes Pool. 4-8-62. Bert had started on the railway at Bromsgrove in 1927 before moving to Evesham and Monument Lane. Copyright T J Edgington.

92079 leaving Blackwell in August 1963 showing the catch points and the crossing which appears to have been taken out of use. Norman Fox.

Three panniers at Blackwell in June 1963. Is that a young fireman or an enthusiast having a ride? Norman Fox.

NUR contribution card belonging to Darryl Lucas showing me as Branch Secretary.

NATIONAL UNION OF RAILWAYMEN
CONTRIBUTION CARD

Name .... D. LUCAS.

Address ....

....

Head Office No. ....

Branch No. ....

National Insurance No. ....

Branch ....

Branch Meets at ....

....

Every ....

Branch Secretary .... P. J. WALLAC

Address ... 16, FOX LANE

HILL TOP

BROMSGROVE.

This pencil sketch was done by David Houghton one Sunday in 1963 whilst the main line was closed for engineering work. David was with Driver Fred Bourne and with nothing much doing he sat down on the rail of the up goods and drew this picture.

"Bromsgrove Banker"

Gordon Russell. Alan Spencer collection.

48095 on a down goods at Blackwell in July 1964. Norman Fox.

44137 approaching the cutting at Blackwell. Cecil Ord collection.

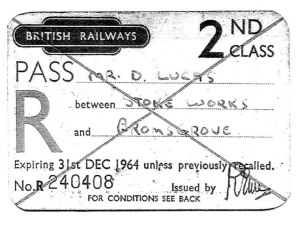

BRITISH RAILWAYS

PASS MR. D. LUCAS

2ND CLASS

R

between STOKE WORKS

and BROMSGROVE

Expiring 31st DEC 1964 unless previously recalled.

No. R 240408   Issued by

FOR CONDITIONS SEE BACK

BRITISH TRANSPORT COMMISSION
(BRITISH RAILWAYS)   B.R. 87156

WESTERN REGION

BICYCLE

PERMIT No. 121053

TO ALL CONCERNED

The Bearer D. J. LUCAS

TRAFFIC _____ Department
has permission to take a bicycle with him,
free of charge, when travelling to, from
or on duty between

STOKE WORKS

and

BROMSGROVE

This permit is issued on the condition
that the Commission is relieved of all
liability for any loss, damage or delay of
or to the bicycle or its accessories which
may occur. It must be produced when
required by the Commission's officials, and
returned to the issuing officer immediately
after its expiry or withdrawal.

NOT TRANSFERABLE.

Valid (unless previously
withdrawn) until 31 DEC 1964

Issued by For J. POWER

Getting to work.

By the sixties some men had cars and motorbikes and the requirement for living close to the shed was relaxed. If you could get to work by train it was possible to have a free ticket and one for your bike too as it was not always possible to go both ways on the train. These are tickets belonging to Darryl Lucas which he made good use of from his home near Stoke Works station until it closed.

D6938 pulling out behind a
train in 1964. Alan Spencer
collection.

The cab of one of our first diesels.
Keith Hargreaves collection.

A fine bunch of men sitting outside the new cabin about 1965. Bert Halfpenny on left then Donald McHarg, Alan Spencer, myself and Gordon Russell. Alan Spencer collection.

Brand new engines at the coal stage, plenty of coal still. Alan Spencer collection.

Four panniers lined up outside number one road of the shed in 1964, 8403 nearest camera. Norman Fox.

D6922 at Blackwell c1964. R S Carpenter Photos.

Bromsgrove _____ M.P. Depot _____ BRITISH RAILWAYS Western Region _____ B.R. 32711/9

ALTERATIONS TO ENGINEMEN'S ROSTERS ON Saturday **DAY** 26/9/ 19 64

Driver	Fireman	On Duty	Turn/ Dia. No.	To Work
Wheeley S	Stokes I	12.5	Bank	
	Baker G	12.5	Cape	
Mayler B	Hinett H.	6.0	Shed	
Yeates E	Wallace P.	7.20	Bank	
Randell V	Houghton D	8.5	Bank	
Bourne I.	Russell G	8.5	Bank	
Stainton D.	Taylor G	12/17	T607	
Pidgeon G.	Hargreaves K	3/0	Bank	
Halfpenny B	Allen R	3/0	Shunt	
Smith S	Trath J.	3/14	T606	
Richardson J.	Griffith R.	4/5	Bank	To Shed after Milford Haven Gt has passed.
Bishop C.	usher S.	10/40	Bank	To Shed after Positioning Paper Van.
	Sunday. Sept 27TH 1964			
Wheeley S	Stokes I	12.5	Bank	
Randell V	Butler a	8.5	Bank	
March H	Miller D	4/5	Bank	

Roster alterations September 26 and 27.

	Monday - Sept 28 - 1964			
Gregson T.	Houghton	12.5	Bank	
Newman T	Steven C	12.30	Bank	
Yeates E	Windrum G	1.5	Bank	
Rudge L I.	Underwood N	3.59	T604	
	Taylor G	8.0	spare	
Halfpenny B	Downs W.	8.20	Bank	
Randell V	Butler a.	8.35	Bank	
Cliff I	Richardson W	8.35	Bank	
		9.10		
Richardson J	Griffith R	12/17	T607	
March H.	Stokes I	2/1	T606	
Hollingshead	Lucas D	4/35	Bank	
Pidgeon G	Allen R	4/40	Bank	
Miller D	usher S	4/40	Bank	
Bourne I	Spencer a	4/40	Bank	
Baker G	Gibbon R	8/27	T609	
Prichard R	Hargreaves K	8/51	T610	
Suckling R		9.0		Pass to Worcester per 11.34 for
Russell G		9.0		Diesel Training.
Harg Mc		8.0		Diesel
Wheeley S		8.0		School
				a. Cox.

The last Alterations to Enginemens Roster to be posted at the shed.

8415 on shed after closure. A nice shot of the refuelling apparatus for the Garratt too. I think the writing says "Take a good look because this one is the last". The wagon behind the engine was the ash wagon and the one on the left was the coal wagon. Also visible is the rack for fire irons. Paul Troth.

Driver Bill Hardy and Alan Spencer at Blackwell in 1965. Alan Spencer collection.

D 6922

driving in May and June. The first week was main line work with Jim Bradley as my mate and the rest of the time a mix of mainline, bank and shed.

We had a lot of young firemen in those days some of whom didn't stop very long as they were lured by the big money at Garringtons or The Austin or their girlfriends didn't like them working shifts. Here are a few I had the pleasure of working with that summer. Keith Nicklin, Ken Lammas, Derrick Harris, Brian Carpenter, Mike Vallender, John Walker, Ken Simmonds, George Manning, Hughie Green and Hughie McGinn. I also had some Saltley firemen, Mahon, Carpenter and Lammas and others whose names I didn't record. Some of these would have been replacing men who were away on national service for two years like I had been.

There were not many fireman that I didn't get to work with but some that I remember were Tim Healey, Brian Delves, Ted Riddell, Peter Hall and a few of the older firemen such as Norman Minett a passed fireman, Cyril Rutter, a good boxer and Charlie Berwick who played for Bromsgrove Rovers.

In August our own 9f must have been in shops as we were borrowing engines from Saltley. I was driving 92136 and 92138 for five days at the end of August. She had still not returned by October as I was driving 92139 on a couple of days with Geoff Barnes as my mate.

On 20th October Trevor Evans was my mate on the bank for one trip with 8402. Trevor was the son of Driver Charlie. Both Trevor and Charlie have passed on but they are still close to the Lickey and if you visit the graveyard at St Godwalds you will recognise their graves as they both have 58100 on the headstones.

92079 was back by the following month as I fired her with Fred Bourne on the 17th and did just two trips.

I was firing for Joe Ashfield on the 26th. Booking on at 5-35am and working to Up Sidings. The rest of the week I continued to work to Up Sidings but with Sam Smith so it would have been a quiet few days.

I had done quite well for driving turns during the year having got to 287 in total, which meant I had a rise in pay, I went on to complete another 20 making a total for the year of 138.

The Salto

A regular job that we had at Bromsgrove for many years was Turn 27 for which we were now booking on at 1-40pm. The time of the job had moved slightly over the years from 2-00pm then 1-45pm and now 1-40pm, a time that remained until the job finished in 1964. This is a typical job when I was driving earlier in the year with Sid Usher as my mate.

The date was 14th January and our engine 43484 had been prepared for us. We had two 3f's of our own, 43186 and 43762, but this was a Saltley engine. Ray Lucas was often our guard and he would arrive early so when we climbed on the engine it was to find the backhead cleaned and the coal brought forward in the tender. With our guard accompanying us on the footplate we left the shed tender first and proceeded down the straight to the South and waited for the signal to let us out onto the goods and down to Stoke Works.

We usually went down this way so we were chimney first going up the bank, if it had been the wrong way round we could have turned it on the turntable behind the South box. We picked up our train here, salt and empty mineral wagons, and returned to Bromsgrove where some more wagons were added. These may have included the sludge tender that resided at the back of the shed and was filled with all the sludge from the water softening plant. We now had a decent train of 41 wagons and with two bankers headed up the bank. Sometimes we would leave the train at Washwood Heath but on this occasion we continued on to Bromford Bridge. From there it was light engine, tender first to West End, the down sidings at Washwood Heath. We picked up our train of 24 wagons there and headed south. After stopping for a banker we proceeded up Camp Hill bank and on towards Bromsgrove. We didn't finish there however as we had salt wagons and some coal for the salt works at Stoke Works. Leaving our train there it was light engine back to Bromsgrove and on to the shed where we left our engine for someone else to dispose.

1958

It is difficult to tell from my diary who my mate was for this year as I spent some weeks with Harry Hinett, Jack Bishop, George Stanley and Ted Bird as well as odd days with most of the others. Ted was a nice quiet chap who of course had the nickname of Dickie, he was another of the flat cap brigade and I think he lived until the age of 90.

In February I had six days with Harry Hinett when we had a Crab every day to Up Sidings. This was either 42763 or 42825. With the Crabs being one of my favourite engines I would have enjoyed that week.

On the Friday 28th I booked on at 6-15 instead of my usual 7-00 and had Bob Burman as my mate before taking up my proper turn with Harry Hinett. I remember Bob well but I think this was the only time we worked together. He would be about 21 at this time a quiet round faced young man whose elder brother Peter had been in my class at school. They lived not far from me up Rock Hill. The following day I booked on early again but my diary says I had no fireman.

I had a driving turn, my 29th, on 4-5 Bank on the Sunday with another young fireman Norman Malpas. We did three trips with 8405.

In March 9455 was at Bromsgrove and I drove her for a couple of days with John Gilder and Hughie Green as my mates. I also had driving turns on 8427 which was on loan to us from Worcester.

An unusual engine appeared on 9th April when Jack Bishop and I had 75061 on a job to Up Sidings. A couple of days later, when with Jack and 48351, we worked to Up Sidings. We were then probably taking the engine to Saltley shed as my diary says in collision with LE off shed.

On 22nd April I attended an LDC meeting so I wonder what was going on. I don't remember the date when I took it on but I must have been the secretary at that time. LDC stood for Local Departmental Committee and it was a bit like shop stewards would be in a factory. Perhaps it was to do with changes after we had come under the Western Region in February. We may have lost some work and that is why I had been put back into the bank link. Our shed code had also changed and we were now 85F.

In the week ending 27th April I was booked on the 1-40pm Salto job with Jack Bishop but I had a couple of driving jobs the first being a 3-20pm bank job with Barry Troth and 47308. The Salto didn't run on a Saturday and Jack and I were on the 4-05pm bank job with 92079. On the Sunday I had a driving turn with Alan Waldron as my mate. This was the 4-05 shift again with 8402 and we only did one trip. I never had Alan as a mate again and like a lot of the other young men he left the railway. Talking to

Ian Tipper during the writing of this book Ian asked me if I knew an Alan Waldron as after being made redundant Ian went to work at the Austin and had worked with Alan. Alan had an interesting tale to tell. He had a neighbour who worked for a brewery and they were about to open a pub called The Lickey Banker. Knowing Alan had worked on the bankers at Bromsgrove he was the obvious choice to open it which he duly did.

The 14th and 15th of May with 43932 and 43989 had Jack Bishop and I working the 10-52am Kings Norton-Westerleigh. I was conducting but I'm not sure why. It may have been after Jack had failed his medical and been put back causing his road knowledge to lapse.

Meanwhile a new engine had arrived in the form of 5226. This was a 2-8-0 tank which was more powerful than a Jinty or pannier but not equal to two so didn't really fit in and could only be classed as one. Why they sent us this I don't know but she remained with us for some time. She was designed to burn Welsh coal and didn't seem to like the hard Derbyshire coal that we had from Williamthorpe, Blackwell and Shirland which she burnt very quickly.

After firing her on the 16th May with Jack Bishop I drove her for the first time on the 29th with Les Wood. For some reason this engine was nicknamed Polyphemus. My mate Les, who would be about 23 at that time, was from a railway family as his Dad was a ganger and lived at Blackwell.

I continued my European holidays when I went to Switzerland in June but on my return I was put back into the bank links the following month.

August Saturdays were a busy time on the bank and after being on 92079 all week with George Allen we did eight trips on the afternoon and evening of the 16th with 47276.

On September 8th Wilf Vallender and I had 47422 on the bank, on loan from Gloucester I think.

A 7-00am start on 26th September had Charlie Evans and I taking 3186 and 7422 light engine to Gloucester. 7422 was a Barnwood engine so perhaps we were towing it back home, I don't remember. That was the third of four days when we worked light engine, the other days we went to Bournville.

1959

This year I was mainly working on the bank so we must have lost quite a bit of work when we came under the Western, perhaps they didn't like us Midland men.

My first driving job this year was not until April, on the bank with Mike Metcalf. We still had 5226 but 92079 went to works around the end of March and we had 92231 as replacement, it was one of the later engines fitted with a double chimney. I didn't get to drive her until 16th July with Brian Dipple as my mate.

August 8th was a typical busy Saturday and I was on 8-05 bank with Bill Bozward. We started the day with 8406 but exchanged her for 8401 by the afternoon. With all the passenger trains about returning from the south west we had eight engines banking, six panniers, Polyphemus and 92231. Most trains were hauled by Stanier Black Fives, Standard Fives or Jubilees but anything could turn up at these busy times. We had already done five trips when 92164 came up shortly after 3-30 and we banked it together with 8404. Our relief had already booked on by the time we got back to the South and we booked off at 4-35 leaving our relief to bank a train straight away.

I had three weeks on the shunter in July and August with Ted Allen and Ted Guy. After starting a fourth week on the shunter with Ted Allen I sprained my ankle and was off work for three weeks. When I returned to work on 14th September it was with Ted Guy on the shunter again but with a pannier number 8400 instead of the usual Jinty.

On 6th October there was a LDC meeting with Mr Sidwell but no details of what it was about. Whatever it was we probably didn't agree with management's proposals, they wanted to find ways to cut jobs and we wanted to preserve them.

From 7th to 10th October George Dyer and I had a different pannier to normal as 8427 was helping out on loan again from Worcester and later on 2nd November it was the turn of 8496. Being a small depot we didn't have many spare engines but would often borrow one when required. If we didn't have enough engines there would be delays to trains.

I had been having driving lessons once a week since July and after getting some experience of driving round Redditch with my brother David

I took my test on the 1st December. As you can imagine I was over the moon when told I had passed especially as I had already splashed out on a new Morris van registration XUY 687.

I was now able to leave my bike in the shed and ride to work in comfort which I did on Christmas Day this year when booked on 7-00am spare. However I was not required and finished at 11-00 and was back home in plenty of time for Christmas lunch.

It was a busy end to the year with between 6 and 7 trips on the last four days with 8401 and driver Jack Bishop.

Rate of pay 204/- when firing and 216/6d when driving.

My last weeks wages for this year were shown as £15-1-4d.

1960-64

MY DETAILED diaries and driving log books have run out so from now on I will have to do a bit of head scratching. I think things were much the same as in 1959 and I was still in a bank link which included the Stoke job, the night goods and a few main line jobs. Two of these jobs were 4-28am and 4-29am and so I would often get out of these by swapping turns. One of them was working a parcels train from Bromsgrove to Gloucester. Another turn was 11-47am. From my 1961 diary which doesn't contain too much detail I see I did work the 4-29am job one day with 44265 but the rest of the week I was on 8-05 bank. There are a couple of days that says Redditch but I can't remember. One shift was from 2-00pm until 10-40pm and the other 8-05pm until 10-40pm. I didn't sign Redditch so perhaps they were short of firemen and I was sent over. I think we sometimes went over to cover the shunter in the yard. When the engine at Redditch was due for washout we would sometimes take a replacement up to Barnt Green and swap over with the Redditch men. While on the Salto on April 21st we came off the road but it doesn't say where. 92079 was still at Swindon at the beginning of the year but when she finally arrived back she had lost the headlamp.

Also in 1961 on 3 November the Queen Mother stopped at Bromsgrove to visit the Blind School. It was possibly on this occasion when the firemen were instructed to clean their engines so they looked respectable when the royal train passed by. Only the one side was cleaned so for some time we had engines running around that were clean on one side and dirty on the other.

During this period the night goods finished, we had been working this job for many years sometimes it was a 9-30pm job and for a long time we booked on at 8-35pm. Our engine would have been prepared for us and our train had been made up by the afternoon shunter and would be trailing back through the goods shed and down towards the bank engine sidings. We would leave the shed and back down from the station into the yard and be coupled up to the train. The bankers, usually two but sometimes three would gain access to the yard from the ashpit by reversing in turn up Spion Cop and buffering up behind us. When we had the road whistles would be exchanged and we would set off out of the yard and through the station. When we were in the station the bankers would be just approaching the goods shed which they would pass through before leaving the yard. What a sight this was, a train being banked through a goods shed, I don't suppose anyone ever took a photo of us as most enthusiasts would have gone home by this time of night.

Barry Troth remembers an incident with this train when he was on one of the three bankers and when they were entering the platform they were given a red light by Gilbert Williams as the train had parted. Whether the shunter had forgot to couple the wagons or whether it was mischievous children we don't know but it was not the first time this had happened.

In 1962 a familiar sight and sound disappeared from Bromsgrove when the wheel tappers were made redundant. They had a little cabin down the straight between the shed and the South which was now redundant.

Early in 1963 David Houghton re-joined us from Redditch. David had started as a cleaner at Bromsgrove in 1959 and after being passed out as fireman in 1960 moved to Redditch in 1961. A couple of months later Gordon Russell also joined us from Redditch, Gordon had started on the railway at Redditch as a cleaner in 1947 and was now a passed fireman on the top rate of pay as he had completed over 300 driving turns at Redditch mostly on passenger jobs. Gordon's father in law was Tom Grindley who had been a fireman at Bromsgrove before moving to Redditch. Tom had started his railway career at Crewe. David was with Ernie Yeates for a couple of months until replaced by Gordon. David then teamed up with Trevor Gwynne for the rest of the year.

The talk in the cabin was sometimes about the diesels that were appearing in other parts of the country and how long it would be before they came our way. We didn't have too long to wait. With the Lickey being the steepest main line in the country it was used to test new designs of diesel and seeing the loads that they could take gave us little hope for the future. It was also rumoured that the wagon works were to close which would mean a loss of work for us and redundancy for my Dad. Eventually diesels started to appear on the expresses but they still stopped for a banker. Some of these expresses would get away from us at Bromsgrove and we didn't always catch up, sometimes it was best to just follow on behind. Not all the expresses were hauled by diesels as there were quite a few failures where steam would deputise and there was still plenty of steam on freight so we were kept busy.

92079 went away in August 1963 and we had a number of different locos as replacement. One of these was 92223 which worked for a few months before being withdrawn with a cylinder problem and stored behind the shed on number 1 Traffic Road one of the three Traffic Roads from which 9F's were prohibited. Its replacement was 92230 which became the last 9f that we had. 92223 was involved in an accident while it was at Bromsgrove when crewed by Ernie Yeates and Gordon Russell. After banking a train and dropping back at Blackwell the train came to a stand as they were down the nick. The 9f went into the back of the train and the brake van was badly damaged and the guard injured. It was later decided to reinstate 92223 and send it to Swindon for repairs but during its time at the back of the shed a bird had nested in the tender so it was not until the eggs had hatched and the birds flown away that it was pulled out and placed on number three shed road to be lit up. This was done by Richard Gibbon around June time and it eventually returned to service at Tyseley.

Also in August an English Electric, D6860, was tested on the bank and being successful it paved the way for them to be introduced as bankers the following year. This was one of a number of diesels that had been tested on the bank in the last year or so. The usual practice was for a banker to follow the train up the bank in case it got stuck but they never did.

When new loading regulations started the expresses would take twelve coaches on their own even though they were hampered by the 40mph through the station. Heavier trains would still have to stop, this was often on summer Saturdays and a lot of extra trains were still steam hauled. Jim Core was our Shedmaster at this time after taking over from Joe Wilkins who had moved on to Bristol Barrow Road. Jim's full name was a rather grand Royal Albert Core.

Alan Spencer started on the railway in 1963, he lived in Redditch and before he bought a motorbike would often cycle to work, I think he had the longest journey of any at that time. Here is an interesting story from Alan's diary. Wednesday 22nd July 1964:

> *On Duty 14:40*
>
> *Prepare 8405*
>
> *15:45 Extra Bank*
>
> *The 9F was on shed on Wash out.*
>
> *At 16:20 6M57 arrived headed by a Single Class 33 (6548), Fawley – Bromford Bridge (Load 26 x 4 wheelers) Approx. 790 Tons*
>
> *The Signaller at Bromsgrove South, pulled the Bottom GS (Ground Signal) off and 4 Panniers went out (Myself and Bert Halfpenny on the 3rd), as the GS did not revert to Danger the other two followed, as there had been no whistle from the Class 33 to indicate how many assistant Locos he required.*
>
> *The Oil Train started away following the Home signal being cleared, and speed on the Incline reached about 20 mph. At Blackwell we were sent right over the top points, to return us to the Banker Siding. Whilst entering the siding, the rear loco was still trying to push us in, my mate saying how much more room does he want. I looked back and forth and said "OMG, there are 6 of us".*
>
> *Meanwhile at Bromsgrove South the Signaller was looking for two lost bankers, and trains were arriving with no assistance in sight. We were quickly dispatched from Blackwell.*

Before we get to the end of steam I had better explain how the bank was worked so the following is a typical trip by an engine that was standing second.

Standing Second

It is 7pm on a sunny Wednesday evening in June 1964. We are at the Banker coal stage at Bromsgrove South at the foot of the Lickey Incline.

Our loco is 84xx Pannier tank No 9453 and we are standing second of five Panniers and the "Big-un" 9f, 92230 for the next train requiring a banker. All trains were assisted on the climb of the incline in the days of steam except for the occasional very lightly loaded train.

A Midland 4f runs by on the Up Goods loop with a long string of 55 empty mineral wagons. We wait to see how many bankers are required, but the ground signals (known as Dummies to the crews) remain at danger. Five minutes later we find out why, when a Black 5 runs by on the up Main line with a fully fitted train of banana vans. The train consists of around 40 vehicles and would probably require two Panniers. The 84xx's are rated at one unit each and the 9f is rated as two units. The bankers take turns in strict rotation with the 9f used for trains requiring two or more providing it is its turn. In this case, it is the pannier's turn for two if this train so requires. With both of us on the footplate, we get ready just in case. Check the water level in the gauge glass and with the rear dampers open and blower turned on to draw the fire, about half a dozen shovels of coal are added to "liven things up" in readiness. The bottom Dummy drops to the off position for the main line. (There are three Dummies sitting vertically. The bottom one takes you to the far right which in this case is "Up Main", the middle one indicates "Up Goods" and the top one straight on to "The Ashpit"). The first pannier moves off and the dummy remains in the clear position indicating that we are also required. As long as the dummy remains in the "off" position, the bankers must follow the others behind the train. The Steam brake is applied to enable the handbrake to be released and the reversing lever is pushed forward from mid to forward gear. Steam brake off and regulator open, steam hisses from the cylinder cocks to clear any water from the cylinders and are almost immediately closed to enable good visibility. Away we go following the first banker up to the train, looking behind to check that a third has not followed us out.

The first banker buffers up to the brake van and the firemen on both bankers look out for the "Up Main" home signal at the front of the train to clear. They will both shout right away to their drivers and if all is well, the fireman of the first banker will pull the whistle chain in a "Crow Call" (cock a doodle doo). Seconds later the Black Five on the front answers and the driver of the first banker opens the regulator to "lean against the train" and waits for the train to move. Once on the move, the first banker gives a toot on the whistle to tell the second banker that he is in full contact with the train. Now it is our turn and we carefully catch the first banker and "open up". By now we are doing around 20mph and the driver of the first banker eases his regulator to enable him to "Notch up" or alter the cut off of his loco. (Whilst he is carrying out this manoeuvre, we are keeping him against the train as we "NEVER" couple to either the train or each other). He will now open up to second valve of the regulator and we will then carry out the same procedure ourselves. Whilst doing this we occasionally lose contact but it is relatively easy to reconnect with the train and then open up ourselves. It is important that these manoeuvres are carried out in this sequence to avoid a rough ride for the guard and the chance of breaking a coupling in the train. All of the banker crews know what the others are doing.

(At night, the fireman on the first banker will keep his firehole doors closed until his driver has started the train and will then open them so that the firelight shining on the bunker windows will indicate to the following driver that it is safe to catch up and start pushing. This applies to successive bankers until all are safely in contact with each other and the train). Also at night, (unlike in daylight hours) the 9f always goes behind the train first on a train requiring three or more bankers. The reason for this is that the tail lights of the bankers are always mounted on the right-hand side of the locos and the 9f (unlike the panniers) is driven from the left hand side of the cab therefore rendering a Pannier tank invisible. (Also, catching the train in the dark with a big loco like a 9 would be quite risky and could result in a "rough shunt" for the poor old guard).

Back to the trip in hand on this lovely sunny evening, we are now approaching Bromsgrove Station and signal box at the foot of the incline and the load is now being felt. Under St Godwalds bridge right at the start of the incline we begin the two track section as far as Blackwell. Our speed has dropped from around 25/30 mph to 20 mph and should (all being well) remain around this speed all the way to the summit at Blackwell.

We are now well onto "The Bank" and the fireman adds another eight to ten shovels of coal and checks the water level and steam pressure. The safety valves of an 84xx are set at 225psi and at present the pressure gauge is showing just over 220psi. With steam pressure rising, now is the time to turn on the live steam injector to add water to the boiler. Whilst on the incline, the water gauge gives a false reading due to the angle of the loco and care must be taken to keep the water near the top of the gauge so that when the loco gets onto the level at Blackwell, and the level reading drops to the "true" reading, it does not drop out of sight in the glass. If this happens and the firebox crown becomes uncovered, fusible lead plugs in the firebox crown will melt (these are fitted to prevent serious damage to the boiler, plus the risk of explosion in such circumstances) and steam and water will blast into the firebox and hopefully put out the fire. This would render the loco (and the fireman) a complete failure and could cause serious damage to the firebox.

We are now passing under the Finstall Road Bridge and past Finstall cemetery. Looking out of the fireman's side to check that the "Automatics" (colour light signals) are off, the fireman calls out to confirm this. We are now climbing out of the cutting and onto a high embankment with a long row of Bungalows to the right and fields to the left. A heavily loaded loose coupled coal train passes on the down with a Stanier 8f at its head. There are around fifty loaded wagons behind the loco and the driver has his hands full. After five more minutes and half a mile further on we cross the main Bromsgrove to Redditch road (this is long before the modern dual carriageway bypass was built) and approaching the halfway point of the climb. To the right is Caspidge Farm and to the left are views over Bromsgrove two miles away and the Clee hills in the distance. We are now crossing over Pikes Pool Lane which, to the left immediately turns sharply to the right to follow the railway, which continues on a "walled" embankment directly above the road. There are a number of cars parked in the layby with their occupants out of their cars watching the proceedings above. Friendly waves are exchanged with the crews as we pass by. The ground on the right has now come up level with the line and in a small copse, is a small brick reservoir, which is provided to store water for the loco supply at Bromsgrove. At present, the pool is covered with chickweed which a family of Mallard ducks are enjoying. To the left we are passing Pikes Pool far below both the railway and the road. Another 100 yards further and the lane now veers away from the line. At this point is the "Back un" (distant colour light signal) for Blackwell another ¾ of a mile further on. At a point a few yards before the road veers away, is a set of sprung catch points which are provided to prevent a runaway from heading back to Bromsgrove. Why they are positioned at precisely this point is unclear, except to purposely give the banker crews a heart attack if they are pushed back by a broken train. The consequences of derailing at this point would probably mean a pile of bankers and wreckage in Pikes Pool Lane. Personally, I think that the steps that the "Banker" crews would take in such a situation would be GREAT BIG ONES in the opposite direction!

We continue to make steady progress, with firing taking place every few minutes and the injector used to keep the water level at a satisfactory height, but not high enough to cause the loco to start priming (causing water to be carried over into the cylinders). The strong exhaust beat of both of the panniers is drawing the fires and therefore keeping the steam pressure up to "the mark". All Great Western locos were built to provide a strong exhaust to enable welsh coal (a very soft tar coal) to be burnt. This was good steaming coal, but needed a strong draw to enable air to be drawn through the stodgy fire. All the different railway companies built their locos so that they were best suited to the coal supplies in their areas and this often explains the difference in the exhaust beats on their locos.

A quick check that the droplets of cylinder oil continue to rise up the sight glasses of the lubricator and thus providing the cylinders with sufficient lubrication confirms that everything is ok. We are now approaching Vigo (a foot crossing with access for service vehicles to approach the railway). The railway bridge over the Burcot Lane at this point has no provision for pedestrians to pass under safely and is the reason for the foot crossing over the railway. More often than not, the vehicle access is occupied by courting couples' vehicles, with many a red face witnessed by the crews when we slip by unexpectedly when returning to Bromsgrove.

We are now within sight of the top with a long row of poplar trees on the right. These cause all sorts of problems in the autumn leaf fall, especially if accompanied by an easterly wind. You would be amazed how many leaves land on the rails and even more amazed at the lubricating effect this can have on the driving wheels of a locomotive. Many times in the autumn, trains will slip to a stand at this point within a hundred yards of Blackwell summit. The guard is then required to walk back and protect the train and then request extra bankers.

We have no problems of this kind this evening and by now; the train engine is over the summit. Speed rapidly increases as more of the train gains level ground. We will now give him a final shove through the Station and as we pass Blackwell Signal box, I will put the blower on and close the regulator leaving the first banker to continue pushing for a short distance more. My fireman closes the dampers and with the boiler nearly full, he turns off the injector. The signalman has indicated that we are to cross over "this end" and we therefore brake to a stand. There are three options for bankers to cross to the down line. The first is sometimes used when banking locals that are booked to stop in Blackwell station. We can then use the trailing crossover on the brow of the incline to cross onto the down line behind the train. The second point is the one we are about to use which is situated just to the north side of the signalbox. The third point is a quarter of a mile further on at Linthurst where a banker layby is provided between the up and down main lines to "hold" the bankers when the down line is occupied.

The ground signal is cleared for us to cross the road so we wait for the other banker to join us. My fireman winds on the handbrake and I move the reversing lever to the reverse position as the other guy buffers up to us. A pop on the whistle and he begins to push us across to the down line and onto the bank. Another loose coupled freight has just set of down the bank after having the wagon brakes "pinned down" and we will follow a hundred or so yards behind. We await the "calling on arm" to clear which will allow us to follow the train down under a "C" indication (which stands for caution). If the line was clear, we would be given the same signal but with a "W" indication for warning. The weight of the other banker against us on the incline ensures that he does not require any power on and we coast down the incline with my fireman controlling the speed and distance behind the freight with the handbrake only.

We are passing Pikes Pool when the 4f with its 55 empties "wheezes" past on the up line. Watching the couplings, we count around eighteen wagons before the couplings become slack and the buffers are now in contact indicating that the bankers are now taking the weight of the rest of the train. When the end of the train finally comes into sight, we find that it is the 9f, 92230 that is taking the strain and judging by the thunderous roar as it passes, Sid Hollingshead must be driving.

As we approach Bromsgrove distant signals, we note that the freight is routed onto the Down Goods. We ease our speed to give him time to clear and manage to arrive at the Station box home signal just as it clears for the Main line through the station and onwards to Bromsgrove South. Through the station the track levels out and with the starter signal clear, the banker behind us applies power to ensure we do not become separated. This he does all the way past Bromsgrove South box to just beyond Newton Bridge where we come to a stand in readiness to cross over to the ashpit. There are again three "Dummies" stacked vertically and as before, the top one indicates far left which in this case is our ashpit siding. At this point we separate and follow the other engine across the Up Main, Up Goods and onto the ashpit. Time for a cuppa I think!

Early in 1964 we began to hear rumours about the shed closing and diesels being introduced and later it was confirmed that closure would take place on September 26th. The first diesel arrived for training, this was D6938 I think. Once the drivers had learnt the basics they were allowed to have a go at banking. Sometimes this was with a steam engine which had to be in front though not coupled.

26th September was the date the shed closed after 124 years. I was on days booking on at 07-20 with Ernie Yeates. There were two diesels and two steam engines banking on the final day one of the 08-05 shifts was steam and the other one diesel and also Bert Halfpenny and R Allen booked on at 3-00pm for shunting, their engine would have been prepared for them by Bert Moyle and Harry Hinett on their last 6-00am shed job. Jack Richardson and Ray Griffiths had a Tankie when they booked on at 4-05pm and were due to go to shed after the Milford Haven Goods had passed. The last engine to go to shed would appear to be 8415 after putting the newspaper van in the yard around 3-40am on the Sunday morning. This engine was manned by Jack Bishop and Sid Usher and they had booked on at 10-40pm.

Diesel years

WITH the closing of the shed voluntary redundancy was on offer and of course some of the older drivers that were coming up for retirement didn't want to learn the diesels and decided to take it. Our Shedmaster Jim Core was to leave and we were to be under the control of Worcester with a Chargehand looking after us at Bromsgrove. Tom Goode got this job and everyone else at the shed received their notice. The fitter, Ray Webley left and went to work at Garringtons, George Stanley went to work on the weighbridge and Jack Daniels retired. Jack was another old LNWR man and I think he came from Monument Lane. He lived in the house built for James McConnell and later occupied by the stationmasters. There were a lot of things that had to be cleared from the shed and so Dennis Faulkner, Pat O'Neil and Ian Tipper remained for six weeks under the control of Tom Goode who moved into the Shedmaster's office.

Everything from the stores was loaded into some vans that were on number three road and sent to Swindon. Some things such as cupboards were broken up and sold as firewood. Fortunately for Ian there were plenty wanting to take redundancy so after the shed was cleared he was retained as a cleaner and after booking on at Bromsgrove travelled to Worcester each day taking with him the correspondence bag containing the driver's tickets etc. After two weeks at firing school at Gloucester in the following January he was passed out by Mr Cole the Worcester Shedmaster and joined us at the South.

With the shed finally cleared out Dennis and Pat left. I don't know what happened to them or Pat's brother Mick who was a coalman at the south.

Although steam had finished on the bank it was not the end for us as we still had jobs that were steam hauled on the main line. These were

T604 3-59am. 7M65 Mondays only pick-up from Bromsgrove to Washwood Heath, we only worked back occasionally, normally it was back passenger on the first down stopper (2M75 06:45 Birmingham New Street-Gloucester) the rest of the week was spent on the bank.

T607 12-17pm 7V37 to Barnwood. We came back with 6M11 18:25 Barnwood-Water Orton.

T606 2-1pm Washwood Heath-Bristol West Depot as far as Gloucester Eastgate, this was normally 40 load of coal. We worked back with the Neath-Whitemoor (5E09) which we relieved on the middle road in Central station. We had all sorts of engines on this train Western, Midland and Standards. At Bromsgrove we were relieved by Bromsgrove men on T609. On a Saturday when arriving at Gloucester we would put the train in at the New Yard and after turning the engine (sometimes tender first) work back to Bromsgrove. The turntable at Barnwood wasn't very big and if we had anything bigger than a Crab we would have to turn on the bigger table at Horton Road shed. Sometimes it was back light engine and sometimes we had a small train which we would back into the up yard at Bromsgrove to form the 3-59am (7M65) on Monday morning. The engine was left on shed.

T609 8-27pm was the Neath-Whitemoor (5E09), if there was a western engine on this job we would come off at Washwood Heath and after turning the engine on Saltley return with it on the 7V25 2-55am Washwood Heath-Gloucester pick-up as far as Bromsgrove. If we had a Midland or Standard engine we were relieved at Landor Street and prepared another engine at Saltley to work the 2-55. Sometimes we would not be finished until 7 or 8am after calling everywhere.

T610 8-51pm was a Mineral train 7V27 which we worked to Gloucester Eastgate or Barnwood. We would then walk to the South to relieve the 5M12 Avonmouth-Bromford Bridge tanks which we worked back to Bromsgrove where we were relieved by Saltley men.

As well as these we continued to shunt the yard with a tank engine borrowed from Worcester. Sometimes this was 8415 an old friend we had used for banking in the past and sometimes it was 4680, 3682 or 9680.

This was a 2-00pm job for a time where we went passenger to Worcester and after walking over to the shed and finding out which engine we had we prepared it and headed for Bromsgrove. We were due off shed at 4-15pm. We did a few hours shunting in the yard with a break for tea and then after taking water it was back to Worcester where we left the engine on the ashpit and returned home passenger. On the Saturday we would book on earlier and relieve Worcester men at Bromsgrove at 11-00am and shunt until around 4-00pm when we would leave for Worcester.

In March and April 1965 if there were Bromsgrove men spare at Worcester they would often bring the engine up as a means of returning home leaving the shed about 5-00am. Ian Tipper recorded in his note book that he did this often with mates Doug Miller and Fred Bourne. On 30th and 31st March with Fred and 8415 he records stopping at Droitwich to throw off some coal for the signalman.

Later in the year this job changed and one of the night shift engines would leave for Worcester at around 5-30am where they would exchange their diesel for a pannier tank which they would take to Bromsgrove for the day shift to do the shunting. The afternoon shift would then return the engine to Worcester and come back to Bromsgrove with a diesel and resume banking.

Drivers and firemen after shed closed

Frank Cliff	Jack Richardson	Gordon Russell
Bert Halfpenny	Harry Marsh	Grahame Taylor
Fred Bourne	Ernie Yeates	Mick Richardson
Trevor Gwynne	Tom Newman	S G (George) Windrum
Sid Wheeley	Pat Wallace	N Underwood
Bill Hardy	Barry Troth	R Allen
Sid Hollingshead	Sid Usher	Darryl Lucas
Doug Miller	Ken Suckling	John Rudge
Derek McHarg	David Houghton	Keith Hargreaves
George Dyer	Chris Stevens	
George Pidgeon	Mick Wood	*Chargehand*
Vic Randall	Alan Spencer	Tom Goode
Charlie Evans	Richard Gibbon	
Reg Probert	Ray Griffiths	*Engine Cleaner*
Les Rudge	Alan Butler	Ian Tipper
Gordon Baker	Fred Stokes	

From September 27th we had enough drivers trained to cover the jobs but there were still some passed firemen who had to be trained. I started my diesel training on October 13th. I think this lasted for about two weeks before you were passed out. The trainers were Eggy Barrat and Tommy Knight. We were passed out by Arthur Bullock an Inspector. The drivers had been trained first and then the passed firemen next. On days on the bank we had three engines in service and in the evening and night there were four. We had our own engines although they were not allocated to us these were D6938-D6941 and D6943 and D6944. As these were our regular engines we had an incentive to keep them clean, the cabs had their paintwork cleaned regularly and we had a long brush for keeping the windows clean. The floors were swept with the same hand brushes as used for years on steam engines and oil lamps were used front and rear as before as at that time we were not allowed to use the electric ones. A van was positioned up by the ashpit stopblock which contained sand that had been dried at Worcester. This was later moved to the headshunt by the cabin after someone ran into it a bit hard. A big difference from steam days was that when more than one engine was banking they were coupled together.

The engines were serviced and refuelled at Worcester in part of the old wagon works were the GWR railcars had been looked after. This was later done at the steam shed after some alterations were carried out to what was the old passenger shed.

From having over 50 sets of men at one time we were now reduced to about 20. As well as being the NUR branch secretary I was also secretary of the LDC and whenever we met management they were always after ways of reducing the number of men and saving money. I went to many meetings, some of them concerning local issues and some national. At one time there was talk of introducing 100 length trains and over a two year period I went to many meetings at Gloucester and Bristol but we always rejected the idea as it would mean a reduction in the number of men.

Over the next few weeks the remaining men passed out on the diesels and we settled down to the new way of working and the easier life. Our new engines even had a urinal in the engine room. Tom Goode remained up at the shed for the time being although we had been promised a new cabin and office. In 1965 the new building was erected next to the old cabin which became the locker room. The new building was actually second-hand as it came from the wagon works but with the benches, tables and desk from the old one we soon made it like home. We still had a coal fire and some coal remained.

Although the base of the coal stage was left in place and remains to this day, the wooden structure was removed.

The diesels proved to be generally reliable but we did get some problems. The residents in the bungalows up Finstall Road thought they could put their washing out now without getting it covered in smuts from the bankers but one of the diesels decided to start throwing out oil and the problem was only fixed after complaints from them. This was not before the sides of the engine were running with oil. There was also a peculiar problem with another engine as when it was started after a period of shut down when the air pressure built up the horn would sound. A flick of the remote horn switch in the A cab would stop this but I don't know whether the problem was ever sorted as the fitters didn't always do their job and many things were written repeatedly in the repair books.

A more serious fault with one of our engines was when travelling to Worcester and going over the AWS ramp approaching Fernhill Heath the engine would shut down. This meant a visit to the rear cab to reset a switch. The fault was finally fixed after some delay to a passenger train one Saturday morning.

In January 1965 a train was being banked by two engines off the goods road when an empty wagon became derailed and caused a right pile up at the bottom of the bank. Vic Randall was driving the first engine with Mick Wood and Ernie Yeates and Gordon Russell the second. It took some time to clear the mess and a breakdown crane was sent from Saltley. There was an enquiry at Bristol and no blame was attached to the bankers, it was put down to the makeup of the train as the empty wagon was between some loaded ones.

There was still some steam on freights at this time and some of the trains hauled by diesels were loose coupled and so still required a banker so we were still doing 3-5 trips on each shift. Most trains had one banker but there were some heavy ones that would have two such as Avonmouth-Bromford Bridge, Milford Haven-Coleshill, Avonmouth-Immingham and Trostre-Leicester and some heavy coal trains too which kept us busy and sometimes a train would require three bankers. Up until January 1965 we were still banking passenger trains regularly as the Gloucester to Birmingham stopping train was still steam but when these finished we were left with just the odd express. There were some DMU trains from Worcester to Birmingham which stopped at Bromsgrove and sometimes when they had an engine not working they would stop at the south for an engine to be attached to the front. We were not allowed to bank these trains from the rear so we had to couple up and connect the vacuum pipes. We did this as quickly as we could so as not to delay the train and at Blackwell we would uncouple and get into the bank engine siding as fast as possible. We would go up the bank a lot faster than they normally did so they probably didn't lose any time. In steam days the guard would have to pull the strings to release the brakes on the DMU as we were working on 21 inches of vacuum and the DMU was 25 inches. Our diesels being Western engines worked on 25 inches but like all Western engines were changed to 21 inches around 1966. Running a bit ahead of myself now the rules were changed in later years, in the 70s I think and we were allowed to bank from the rear without coupling but with a speed limit of 20mph which was never adhered to.

As in steam days we took it in turns and if an engine was kept at Blackwell and returned with another they were soon sorted into the correct order when back at the south.

With the death in 1965 of George Pidgeon we lost one of our senior drivers. George still had a couple of years to go before retirement and never got to enjoy a well-earned rest after many years of hard work on the railway. Many years earlier Alan Pidgeon, George's son would come down and ride up the bank with his dad. Alan was a good cricketer and we would set up a tin can as wickets and bowl to him but we could never get him out.

In March 1965 we had what could have been a fatal accident. I was driving D6944 to Worcester, Keith Hargreaves was sitting in the secondmans seat and also on the engine with us was Grahame Taylor who was on his way back home to Worcester. After leaving Droitwich we had probably got up to about 60mph when there was such a bang when one of the front windows came in along with some bricks. We came to a stand and checked each other to see that we were alright. Keith had come off the worst and had been cut by the flying glass but was more shocked than anything. Walking back to the bridge that we had just passed under we could see that a car had hit the parapet sending loads of bricks onto the line. We protected both lines with detonators and after reporting the incident carried on to Worcester. We returned to Bromsgrove via Abbotswood Jct and the Old Road I think with a different engine as D6944 needed repairing. Once Keith got over the shock he was none the worse for the incident and his cuts soon healed but he does admit to a slight panic attack the next time he went under that bridge which he did shortly after with a steam engine.

On the 12th of April 1965 there was a busy start to the night shift as 4M23 16-50 Herbranston-Coleshill with a sick engine needed three bankers. Two was the normal requirement for this train of liquid gas.

In 1965 we found we were to lose our main line work. These jobs were being changed over to diesel traction and as we didn't know these engines it was a good excuse for the jobs to be taken off us. This meant some more men taking redundancy. We first learned of this when Alan Spencer and I attended a meeting at Furlong House in Nottingham this was a 610 meeting about inter regional freight loss caused by the Reorganisation of freight services on the north east-south west route and there were representatives from Gloucester, Bristol, Saltley, Bescot, Burton, Derby and Nottingham. Being a small depot we had two representatives but the larger depots had four.

After losing these jobs we had spare men and some would travel to Worcester and sit in the cabin there in expectation of a job and some would go route refreshing. Route refreshing was important as it was essential that we still signed the road to Gloucester, Washwood Heath and New St as we still got called upon to assist when engines failed on both passenger and goods. Although Gloucester was normally as far south as we would go with a failure on 20th July 1965 D1725 failed in the down loop at Blackwell, Sid Hollingshead and Alan Spencer were on D6943 and went to assist finishing up at Severn Tunnel Junction, a Saltley Driver Conducted for the last leg from Gloucester.

A steam engine was still being used for shunting at this time as the track in the yard was not deemed suitable for diesels until it had been upgraded. As well as banking the normal mixed goods we had a number of specials carrying pigeons, beer, bananas, cauliflowers and broccoli. The cauliflower train was very heavy and would come up on a Sunday night from Ponsondane. Another train that ran on a Sunday night was one from Bristol to Catterick, 1N58, which was for army personnel only.

A train called The Rabbits was derailed near Dunhampstead on 10th June 1965. 3M25 was hauled by a Class 45 with 12 vans of perishables, including two of Rabbits for Birmingham Bull Ring market. Both roads were closed for 2 days.

The following is our Roster after we lost our main line jobs in May 1965. This was before we had moved to the 24 hour clock. Times like 8.5 and 12.5 are am jobs and 2/30 and 4/5 would be pm jobs. RD was a rest day. The other numbers are turn numbers where for example 1072B would relieve 1072A.

	Sunday	Monday	Tuesday	Wednesday	Thursday	Friday	Saturday
Week 1		8.5 1072B	8.5 1072B	RD	8.5 1072B	8.5 1072B	8.5 1072B
Week 2		12.5 1072A	12.5 1072A.	12.5 1072A	12.5 1072A	12.5 1072A	12.5 1072A
Week 3		RD	RD	4/5 1074C	4/5 1074C	4/5 1074C	4/5 1074C
Week 4		8.5 1073A	8.5 1073A	8.5 1073A	8.5 1073A	8.5 1073A	8.5 1073A
Week 5	4/5 1072C	4/5 1071C	4/5 1071C	RD	4/5 1071C	4/5 1071C	4/5 1071C
Week 6		12.5 1074A	12.5 1074A	12.5 1074A	12.5 1074A	12.5 1074A	12.5 1074A
Week 7		RD	RD	8.5 1074B	8.5 1074B	8.5 1074B	8.5 1074B
Week 8	8.5 1072B	4/5 1074C	4/5 1074C	4/5 1071C	4/5 1072C	4/5 1073B	4/5 1073B
Week 9		8.5 1071B	8.5 1071B	8.5 1071B	RD	8.5 1071B	8.5 1071B
Week 10		12.5 1071A	12.5 1071A	12.5 1071A	12.5 1071A	12.5 1071A	12.5 1071A
Week 11	12.5 1072A	4/5 1073B	4/5 1073B	4/5 1073B	4/5 1073B	4/5 1073B	4/5 1073B
Week 12		Spare	Spare	Spare	Spare	Spare	Spare
Week 13		4/5 1072C	4/5 1072C	4/5 1072C	RD	4/5 1072C	4/5 1072C
Week 14			12.5 1073C	12.5 1073C	12.5 1073C	12.5 1073C	12.5+11/55
Week 15		8.5 1074B	8.5 1074B	8.5 1072B	8.5 1071B	RD	RD
Week 16		2/30 Shunt	2/30 Shunt	2/30 Shunt	2/30 Shunt	2/30 Shunt	2/30 Shunt

Steam finished on the Western Region at the end of 1965 and by this time diesels were allowed to do the shunting in the yard. One of our engines went to Worcester in the morning for servicing and refuelling which was now done in the old steam shed. While this was being done we would usually go and have a walk round the shops and maybe pop into the railway club for a beer before returning in time for our return working.

For this we left the shed around 1-00pm and went over to the yard behind Shrub Hill station where we picked up our train. We called this the Tripper and leaving Worcester with a dozen or so wagons we called at Droitwich where we went into the loop. We put off any wagons for here and shunted the couple of sidings on this side of the line before crossing over to the other side and doing the same there. Sometimes we also went to Berry Hill sidings which were up towards Kidderminster by the coffin factory. The shunter's name at Droitwich was Charlie and we usually had time for a cup of tea with him before leaving for Bromsgrove. Arriving at Bromsgrove we might have time for a little bit of shunting before being relieved by the men that had booked on at 4/5. These men would continue with the shunting before taking the train back to Worcester and returning light engine and continuing the rest of the shift banking.

Late in 1965 we had a surprise when steam returned briefly to banking duty at Bromsgrove. Ian Tipper was spare that day and remembers it well.

On 7th October 1965 I was spare on afternoons, not sure what time I booked on, possibly 3-00 and instead of travelling to Worcester Tom Goode asked me to stop at Bromsgrove as a steam engine was being sent up for banking. One of our engines had been derailed somewhere. I think it must have been some time after 4pm when the engine arrived in the shape of 6947 Helmingham Hall, an Oxford engine. The engine was backed into the bank engine siding along the coal stage and the crew disappeared. Frank Cliff and Mick Wood were the men for this engine and had booked on at 4-05 but they never stirred from the cabin. Sometime later, about five o clock I think, the phone rang and it was a train requiring one banker. I didn't want to miss this so as Frank and Mick left the cabin I asked Frank if I could go with them to which the answer was yes. Bromsgrove had lost its mainline jobs earlier in the year and unless Frank and Mick had had a job at Worcester when they were spare they hadn't been on a steam engine for some months and had not banked with one for over twelve months.

You wouldn't have known it though as they just went about their jobs as if they hadn't been away from a steam engine. Mick put a dozen or so shovels around the box as we left the bank siding and we were soon behind the train. We went up the bank quite well with Mick feeding the fire again and before long we were back at Bromsgrove where we had news that a diesel was on its way. Because of this Frank put the engine on the top by the bike shed. Worcester had been on the phone and I was directed to look after the engine until someone came to collect it. About half an hour later two diesels arrived and one was left for Frank and the other went back to Worcester. So now I was in sole charge of the last steam banker. I just had to keep an eye on the fire and make sure there was some water in the boiler until someone came to collect it. About an hour later a set of men came and took it away. So that was the end of steam banking until many years later.

Two days later on the Saturday we had some more excitement when we were waiting for Flying Scotsman to come up light engine. A down goods, 7V26, ran by with the engine, D40 on fire. The fire brigade were called and a report and photo appeared in the local newspaper.

It was around this time that we managed to get a bit of extra work delivering new engines to South Wales. English Electric type 3' engines were still being built and had to be delivered to Cardiff but because of a lack of men with the traction knowledge in the midlands we got this extra work. After booking on in the morning a set of men would travel to New Street and then make their way to Duddeston Road where they would wait for their engine to arrive. I think it was Sheffield men that we relieved and with the smell of fresh paint in our nostrils we were then off to Gloucester where we were relieved by Cardiff men at Central station. After a cup of tea it was then back on the cushions to Bromsgrove. Some of these engines were in the D66xx series which we later had at Bromsgrove to replace our original engines.

We still had some spare men in 1966 and in the October Old Oak Common were short of men and looking for volunteers to go on loan. Alan Spencer and Chris Stevens took up the challenge and went to live in the hostel by the shed. Chris returned just before Christmas but Alan moved to Southall where he stayed until the following March. While at Southall Alan had his last steam job when he fired Pendennis Castle to

Didcot where there was a handing over ceremony. The loco had been sold and its new owners wanted Didcot to be its base.

With the goods shed closed an oil depot had been built and sometimes we would shunt the tanks such as when D219 arrived on 9th February and D6606 did the shunting. We still had traffic for Garringtons and the Tripper, now worked by Worcester men, would arrive with a variety of locomotives such as D4168 which was on the job on the 10th of February.

On Sunday 12th March all our engines had to have an axle examination so D6607 came up from Worcester to change over with D6608.

We were still getting jobs on the main line due to failures and around midnight on 12th May D1673 Cyclops failed while working 7V35 from Washwood Heath and it was assisted to Gloucester by D6607 which arrived back at 04-10. In the early hours of 12th June D1741 failed on 7V18 and Harry Marsh and Darryl Lucas assisted to Gloucester. D5288 failed at Barnt Green in the early hours of 26th May and D6605 went light engine and put the train inside before returning home. The following month, 11th July, Sid Wheeley and Ian Tipper went a bit further when they took a coal train as far as Stoke Gifford with D6607. These are just a few of the many freight and passenger trains that needed rescuing by us. Apart from Motorail trains we didn't bank too many passenger trains now but the Cornishman did stop for a banker on 4th June when D6607 was on duty. We didn't only bank trains though and on 28th June D17 came up light engine with three traction motors out and so required a banker. This was not an isolated incident as on 18th October D97 also came up light engine and required a banker. It wasn't only up the bank that trains needed assistance either, as it was on this date that D7021 and D7024 went to Blackwell and assisted a train of condemned coaches down the bank.

Darryl Lucas describes an interesting day with Harry Marsh.

On 12th July 1967 Harry Marsh was my mate and with D6608 we came to a stand on the bank when the train engine ran out of fuel. The other two engines came to our rescue and we pushed the train onto the goods line at Barnt Green before returning to Bromsgrove. Our second trip this day was when a train requested two bankers but we were the only one available and had no trouble in achieving

35mph up the bank. On our third trip we noticed the embankment on fire at Finstall, the signal cables were damaged causing a block failure. Our fourth trip was when we had to rescue one of our own engines as D6606 had failed at Blackwell. We brought it back down the bank and left it on the ash pit for the fitters who were coming up from Worcester.

Diesel Hydraulics

We had heard rumours early in 1966 that our engines were to be replaced by Hymeks and these rumours were confirmed when D7007 arrived for banking trials in March. Although the trials were deemed a success it was not until July 1967 that we heard that we were to have the Hymeks and D7011 finally arrived for training at the end of August. We must have started our training earlier in the month though as Darryl Lucas records in his diary on Wednesday 2nd August that with John Rudge driving he took Harry Marsh and me to Worcester on D6605 for Hymek training. I think we were all passed out on the Hymeks by Inspector Jones or Inspector Crabb. We had a number of different engines during training which lasted for about a week but eventually had our own which were D7021-25.

Having our own engines was nice as it gave us an incentive to keep the cabs clean. During September and October as more men were passed on the Hymeks we had a mixture of hydraulic and English Electric engines banking together. By the end of October we had our own Hymeks and all the English Electrics, D6604-D6608, had gone. The main difference with the Hymeks was the gear changing; this happened at around 23mph so it usually occurred as you were going over the top at Blackwell and could sometimes give the guard a snatch and wake him up but was not a great problem. At first the Hymeks were quick off the mark but they were all gradually modified and apart from notch one which gave you power straight away there was a delay after opening the controller. This could make it difficult if a train got away from you at Bromsgrove and great care was needed to avoid hitting the rear of the train. Apart from this I think we all came to like the engines and with no nose in front of you visibility was improved.

On Mon 23 Oct 1967 Philip Marshman started at Bromsgrove having transferred from Westbury. Ian and Richard had already met Phil when together with men from other Western Region depots they had attended a meeting at Bristol. Phil was already familiar with hydraulics as he had worked on many at Westbury. I gave up the job of LDC secretary some months later and Phil took over as chairman, so along with Alan as secretary I think we had the youngest representatives in the country. You had to be 21 to be on the LDC.

A few days later on 27th October an English Electric did some banking again. D7024 had got stuck while banking a heavy train and D6926 was travelling north light engine and was sent up from Bromsgrove to assist. Having left Bromsgrove at 07-10 the train eventually arrived at Blackwell at 07-45.

Although I have no diaries from this period we are lucky in that some of the other men did keep a record of happenings at Bromsgrove. This is an interesting one from Darryl Lucas.

Friday 3 November 1967. My Driver was Harry Marsh on D7021. One note describes one of our banking trips as being "the roughest trip I have ever known" with a comment that we nearly wrecked D7021 (though I did not elaborate on that). However, the more interesting note was that D342, 8Z09, towing dead steam loco's 75002, 75013 and 75006, ran away down the incline out of control passing the Bromsgrove South cabin with "wheels like Catherine wheels!!!

It doesn't mention where it finally stopped but what a final adventure for those 75 standards on their last trip.

On 4th November I was on days and was relieved by Harry Marsh. Harry and his mate Darryl Lucas were to take their engine to Worcester for refuelling but when Harry went to start the engine he found there was no key in the controller, it was in my pocket. Luckily Darryl had a car so a quick trip to my house to retrieve the key and all was well.

On the evening of Friday 24th November an accident occurred at Bromsgrove station when a down freight became derailed and caused extensive damage to the track and platform. A breakdown crane arrived a few hours later hauled by D7067. One of our engines D7024 assisted with the recovery of the wagons and the up line was opened by the Saturday afternoon as Ian Tipper records in his diary banking one train with D7044 on the 16-05 shift.

This was a bad period for derailments as a wagon was derailed at the same spot on Wednesday 29th and down at Cheltenham Lansdowne an engine was derailed on the same day.

During November we all had a day trip to Bristol as we were to be provided with ear plugs for when we had to enter the engine room. All our ears were different so we had to see the doctor to make sure we had the correct ones.

We tried to avoid going in the engine room and preferred to climb down and walk to the other end at Blackwell or if we were coming straight back down it was handy to change ends in the platform and easier for the secondman to change the red shades in the lamps at night.

At the beginning of December one of our engines, D7021 was fitted with a small snowplough.

We had always had cats down at the south and here are a few notes from the diary of Darryl Lucas.

> *Wednesday 17th January 1968. Alan (Spencer) found a kitten in the engine room of D7025. We reckon it must have been there for three days (poor thing). We named him Hymek.*
> *Saturday 27th January 1968. Cat rode on the bogie of D7022 for four trips! We couldn't get him out! Hymek obviously liked Hymeks.*

One of our cats was called Austin after the Longbridge train, not sure why. He had part of his tail cut off by a tank train. Ginger was another feline friend that I remember. George was perhaps named after or by George, he was very docile. On a recent visit to the South by some of my workmates a white cat crossed over the bridge and went down the path to the cabin, perhaps it was descended from one of ours as a lot of kittens were born over the years.

	D15XX BWU	D10XX BWU	D11/199 BWU	D800 BWU	D67XX BWU	D7000 BWU
No Banker	44	43	40	35	29	29
1 Banker	73	72	69	64	58	58
2 Bankers	102	101	98	93	87	87
3 Bankers	131	130	127	122	116	116
4 Bankers	160	159	156	151	145	145

Loading limits for freight trains up the Lickey in 1968. I think BWU stood for Basic Wagon Unit.

At the start of April 1968 it was the turn of a passenger train to fail when 1V46 expired at Blackwell. D7023 worked the train as far as Worcester. It passed Bromsgrove at 19-10 only around 20 minutes late so there had been some quick work in coupling up.

A regular train that required two bankers was 5M12 the Avonmouth to Bromford Bridge tanks that we used to work in the days of steam. For some reason on 2nd May it went with only one banker and with 23 tanks promptly got stuck.

On Tuesday 21st May I was on the afternoon shift with Darryl Lucas as my mate. At 19-00 we were banking a train of empty hoppers and as we went past Vigo the Brush 4 on the front failed. We managed to push the train over the top but as we crested the summit our own engine D7021 reverted to tick over with notch 1 power only as the transmission had overheated and a warning light was showing. As we slowly passed Blackwell signal box, Fred Smith the Signalman came to the window with an instruction for us to push the train through to (Initially) Barnt Green. Still moving, I explained our predicament and told him we would do our best, but may not make it. However, our Hymek kept things moving (just) and in fact, as we passed Barnt Green box we were asked by the Signalman if we would try to keep going to Kings Norton. We were being turned onto the Goods road and at this stage we really had our doubts if we would get there. However, we plodded on at no more than 10mph and eventually reached Kings Norton where two locos had been sent from Saltley. One was to take over the train and the other (D1749) to tow us to Worcester. When we arrived at Worcester, we handed D7021 over to the fitters and were given a blue liveried replacement in the shape of D7040. We returned from Worcester coupled with D1749 which was on its way back to Saltley. We later learned that the fault on D7021 was merely a faulty micro switch, which was easily rectified. It certainly showed what gutsy locos the Hymeks were.

At the end of the month on the 29th the driver of D1720 wasn't taking any chances with 6M69 and 101 units and had three bankers when he left Bromsgrove at 09-50. For some reason on 20th June we never had any of our usual engines and D7000, D7018 and D7052 were banking.

It was a week or so after this that D130 failed between Dunhampstead and Stoke Works on the northbound Devonian, 1N37. We had got our normal engines back by this time and D7021 propelled the train to Bromsgrove where D7023 hooked on the front and took the train to New Street.

Since the end of steam the practice of having a fry up had stopped, on the English Electrics there was a small circular hot plate but it was only good enough to keep a can of tea warm. The Hymeks had something a bit better and when Ian Tipper was my mate in 1968 we decided to have a fry up when we were booked on a ballast job down the old road one Sunday morning. On the Saturday I popped down the road to get some bacon from Tom Godfrey who kept his own pigs, while there I also picked up some free range eggs and together with some mushrooms we were ready for Sunday. As we thought on Sunday morning we had plenty of time to get cooking once we had positioned our train. It wasn't quite the same as when it was cooked on the shovel but it came a close second especially as we were sat enjoying the country air.

Talking of food when we were on the afternoon shift someone would sometimes go up the road to get us some chips for our supper. We had a hotplate and oven in the cabin so it was suggested that we cook our own. Ken Suckling who was often on his favourite afternoon shift became head chef and we would have a nice plate of egg and chips. If a train came up while Ken was cooking someone would stand in for him knowing he would get his reward on his return. Ken's dad was named Edgar and he was a driver at Bromsgrove when I started but left after a couple of years so I never got to fire for him.

At the coal stage c1965 Keith Hargreaves, Darryl Lucas and Ken Suckling left to right standing. Left to right seated are Charlie Evans, Bill Hardy, Vic Randall and Ernie Yeates. Alan Spencer collection.

Fred Stokes at the coal stage c1964. Note the bag has been taken off the column and the long brush used for cleaning the engine windows. Alan Spencer collection.

Trevor Gwynne c1964. Alan Spencer collection.

Keith Hargreaves on approach to Newton Bridge where we parked our cars much to the annoyance of the local farmer sometimes. Keith Hargreaves collection.

A young Mick Wood along with myself and Melvin Williams. Keith Hargreaves collection.

Chris Stevens and myself enjoying a day at the races.

Flying Scotsman seen passing slowly on the up main as the firemen deal with D40. John Rudge (left) and Sid Wheeley look on. Ian Tipper.

*D7023 on the stop block c1969.
Rob Davies.*

*The scene at the top of the bank
after the accident in 1969. Paul
Troth.*

Richard Gibbon before we had our new uniforms. Alan Spencer collection.

Tom Goode with his trusty moped at the South. Alan Spencer collection.

D1746 at Vigo 28-5-70. Chris Fox.

D7022 and D7025 bank D1746 at Vigo 28-5-1970. For many years the bankers were always used with the number 1 or A cab leading up the bank but as this picture shows once we started using them in multiple it suddenly didn't matter anymore. In earlier years if one came up from Worcester the wrong way round it was sent back to be turned on the triangle. Chris Fox.

D177 starting the climb of the bank on 17-7-1971. Chris Fox.

D7022 banking D177 on 1E20 17-7-1971. Chris Fox.

D140 at Bromsgrove 17-7-71. Chris Fox.

7076, 7001 and 7004 at Blackwell dropping back after banking a heavy train in June 1972. Chris Fox.

6971 and 6941, one of our original class 37's, give a final push over the top at Blackwell, 20-4-1973. Chris Fox.

2 class 37's at Bromsgrove banking what looks like a steel train in August 1975. Chris Fox.

37229 at Blackwell with a steel train. Photo taken from banker. Neil Gordon.

37232 and 37205 passing through the bankers siding at Blackwell. Neil Gordon.

37176, 37303 and a failed 37232 in the banker siding at Bromsgrove. Neil Gordon.

47287 at rear, 47100 on the left and bankers 37220 and 37219. Neil Gordon.

47222 which had arrived on an oil train parked near the cabin next to my car. Neil Gordon.

A view taken from the cab of 37047 in the bankers siding at Blackwell showing 47362 heading south with 6V96 on 3-7-86. Neil Gordon.

31212 about to get onto the bank with 6E35 and two bankers. We knew this train as the Cobra. 6-6-86. Neil Gordon.

37223 and 37219 banking 6E35 hauled by 31212 on 6-6-86. *Neil Gordon.*

The day the guard fell out of the train 2-8-85. It's difficult to see but I am looking out as we get under way. I usually hide when I see a camera and that is why there are not many pictures of me. Mick Wood is driving. Neil Gordon.

L to R Kevin Barham, John Rudge, Mick Wood and myself. Author's collection.

Taken after I had banked my last train, 37177 and 37501 (nearest camera) ready for action on the final night. Neil Gordon.

"Hard Work" a picture that won many awards for the photographer William Scriven. Courtesy of Pat James.

21C shedplate.

85F shedplate.

85D shedplate.

When a club and canteen was opened at Garringtons just down the road it was possible to get some food from here if you were stuck and liquid refreshment was also available.

With the route set to be modernised with multiple aspect signalling preparations were being made and on 27th July D1009 ran round its cable laying train at Bromsgrove before returning south.

Thirteen minutes was the sort of time a freight train would take in steam days but a Western class diesel D1007 with only one banker took that long on 20th September with 4M22. The following month when 7M45 came up hauled by D1002 the driver took no chances as it was the leaf fall season and there could be a slippery rail at the top of the bank, he had three bankers when he left at 22-10.

Another failure on bonfire night meant D7022 taking a train as far as Duddeston Road where D20 took over and the failure was deposited on Saltley shed.

Another train requiring three bankers was a train of slack and steel hauled by a Peak on the 16th this was 7M69 which went up the bank at 08-25. A couple of days later on the 18th the mail stuck on the catch points at 03-40 and needed the help of a banker.

We had bad news at the end of the year when it was decided to have only one single engine banking with the other two coupled in multiple. We started this way of working from Monday 2nd December. This unfortunately meant some more redundancies and after January 1969 we were down to just seventeen men. Pat Wallace, John Rudge, Ken Suckling, Darryl Lucas, Richard Gibbon, Mick Wood, Sid Wheeley, Barry Troth, Bert Halfpenny, Fred Bourne, Phil Marshman, Mick Richardson, Jack Richardson, Harry Marsh, Alan Spencer, Reg Probert and Grahame Taylor.

1969 Roster

Sunday	Monday	Tuesday	Wednesday	Thursday	Friday	Saturday
08-05.	08-05.	RD	08-05.	08-05.	08-05.	08-05.
	16-05.	16-05.	16-05.	16-05.	16-05.	16-05.
	00-05	00-05	00-05	00-05	RD	00-05 M
00-05.	Spare	Spare	Spare	Spare	Spare	RD
16-05.	16-05.	RD	16-05.	16-05.	16-05.	16-05.
	00-05.	00-05.	00-05.	00-05.	00-05.	RD
		08-05.	08-05.	RD	00-05	00-05+23-59
	16-05.	16-05.	RD	08-05.	08-05.	08-05.

ENGINES in multiple had been used for banking before this time as we sometimes had a train of tanks up on a Sunday night which required two bankers. With only one set of men on duty the proper procedure was for them to couple up in multiple with the spare engine and bank the train before reverting to a single engine on their return to Bromsgrove. With the pipes being a bit stiff from lack of use and a shortage of time before the train arrived some crews put plan B into operation. This was where we just dropped the coupling on and the driver would drive the lead engine and his mate would drive the other, it was usually dark by now and no one was the wiser so keep it to yourself please! At Blackwell the driver would stop where he was and his mate would change ends and drive back down the bank. This was a slight bending of the rules something that railwaymen had always done to keep the job moving.

Any failures on the main line now would be assisted by the single engine and one of the earliest instances of this came on 4th February when I was on the 08-05 shift with Darryl Lucas as my mate and we assisted a train to Gloucester South after the failure of its Brush type 4. I don't know what the rush was but Darryl drove back in record time.

We had quite a bit of Sunday work at the beginning of the year as preparations were being made for the introduction of the Multiple Aspect Signalling scheme. I was on a ballast working on Sunday 20th April with 7024 accompanied by Darryl. The new signalling became operational on Monday 21st April. From this date the bankers were no longer stabled at the old coal stage but further south on a section of the old up goods line which had been taken out from Stoke Works Junction.

On 6 May 69 Darryl and John Rudge worked to Gloucester when D157 failed with a train of 1364 tons.

On Monday 30th June 1969 there was an accident at the top of the bank when a train carrying some new cars, some container wagons and then mineral wagons loaded with coal came to grief. Two of the container wagons ended up on top of the new cars. There was a van full of cakes and pies and after it was put in the siding at Bromsgrove we were told to help ourselves. The cabin was full of boxes and people were coming from Garringtons and walking over the tracks to help themselves from the wagon. Mr Fred Cole who was the Worcester area manager came up in his car and loaded up but knowing Mr Cole the cakes and pies would have not been all for himself but shared out when he got back to Worcester.

Even though we'd had diesels since 1964 we were still wearing overalls and grease top caps but this came to an end around this time when we were issued with new uniforms and hats. It was also around this time that our firing days finished for good when our old coal stove was removed from the cabin and replaced by an electric heater. Perhaps they didn't want us to get our new uniforms dirty.

On Saturday 6th September 1969 there was a flower show at Garringtons and I managed to find an hour to look at the blooms with my mate Darryl Lucas, there was obviously nothing about.

Towards the end of 1969 Philip Marshman went back to Westbury after a two year stay with us.

All drivers continued to sign the road to New Street, Washwood Heath and Gloucester in case of failures which happened quite often. One of these occasions was on the 16-05 shift on 4th November 1970 when 1945 failed at Stoke Works on 8V89. Ian Tipper who had been made redundant in 1969 still came down for a chat and trip up the bank and was with us in the cabin when the phone rang. My mate was Ken Suckling and we were on the single engine 7001. So Ian joined us when we made our way down to Stoke and coupled up to the loco. We worked the train as far as Hatherley Junction where we put it inside and took the failed loco to Gloucester. By the time we had deposited 1945 on Horton Road shed it was 22-30 so we soon uncoupled and headed for home. My mate would have been getting thirsty by now.

Trains booked bankers in 1969

6M08 23-20 Mx Worcester-Washford Heath 2359-0002.

5M14 19-45 Avonmouth-Derby 0030-0040.

5M91 20-30 Cardiff-Wolverhampton 0151.

3E35 22-45 Fo Q Cardiff-Immingham 0247-0250.

6E87 20-50 Cardiff-Tinsley.

5M12 23-55 Sx Avonmouth-Bromford Bridge 0332-0336.

4M23 20-20 Milford Haven-Coleshill 0425-0428. Q to Tipton or Longport.

4M31 02-15 Q Avonmouth-Nuneaton 0504-0508.

5M72 02-55 So Stoke Gifford-Bescot 0530-0533.

7E07 01-00 Westbury- Donnington 0542-0545.

7E67 03-30 Severn Tunnel Jct- Tinsley. 03-10 So.

4E05 06-05 T ThSo Alexandra Dock-Scunthorpe 0926-0929.

7E70 04-55 T ThSo 02-20So. Alexandra Dock-Normandy Park 0952-1008.

7M62 07-25 Severn Tunnel Jct-Washwood Heath 1029-1032.

7M21 10-35 Worcester-Washwood Heath 1112-1115.

5M20 09-00 Avonmouth-Bromford Bridge.

5M65 07-10So Margam-Washwood Heath 1235-1242.

7M20 1140 Gloucester-Washwood Heath 1301-1313.

7M85 08-15 MWFo Margam-Derby.

3E46 12-50 Sx Cardiff-Sheffield 1512-1515.

5M65 10-00 Sx Margam-Washwood Heath 1532-1547.

7M22 15-42 Gloucester-Washwood Heath.

5N18 14-50 Sx Bristol-Newcastle (Tyne).

6E71 13-55 So Cardiff-Normandy Park. Scunthorpe. 1744-46.

6M11 16-40 So Gloucester-Washwood Heath.

4N55 15-40 Q Shirehampton-Port Clarence 1908-1915.

5M67 15-55 Sx Stoke Gifford-Crewe 1958-2008.

4N29 17-05 Sx Bristol-Healey Mills 2034-55.

4E22 17-10 Q Avonmouth-Immingham 2101-2107.

3E49 18-20 Cardiff-Sheffield.

7M06 19-55 Sx Gloucester-Washwood Heath 2115-2132.

6N28 12-15 TTho MFo Q. Bargoed-South Bank 1832-35.

6N28 12-25 Wo MFo Q. Ystrad Mynach-South Bank 1832-35.

7M45 13-00 Sx Trostre-Leicester 2222-25.

4N14 20-55 MWo Severn Beach-Wilton.

Tom Goode retired late in 1969 and I became Driver in charge for which I was paid six hours pay each week. This was later cut to four when the number of men was reduced. Tom had been responsible for cleaning the cabin, locker room and toilets as well as rosters and correspondence so Barry Troth took over the cleaning role for which he got a small increase in his pay.

On Tuesday 11th November 1969 a Brush failed and with Darryl as my mate we assisted the steel train to Worcester with the multiple, 7022/25.

Oil Leak

Darryl Lucas was my mate when this incident occurred so I will let him tell the story:

> *Something that I found this morning was rather a surprise. I always thought that when the oil leak occurred at around 02.30 on January 1st 1970, that I was with Sid Wheeley. I have however just checked my diary and find that I was actually with Pat on D7021 on 00.05 turn.*
>
> *I do remember that it was a very cold and frosty night and the oil tanks had arrived in the yard about 01.00 and in fact we followed it down the bank after our first trip. When we went our second trip between 02.30 and 03.00, I remember that we wondered where all the "water" was coming from all over the track which we could see in the lights from the yard. I was just about to step in it to press the "RA" plunger when I realised that it was in fact oil. We attempted to warn*

the staff at the oil terminal but it seemed that as soon as they had connected the pipes and turned on the pumps, they had disappeared "somewhere" to resume their New Year celebrations. (I think that when they returned they didn't find much to celebrate).

It appears that when the train was connected to the ground pipeline, one of the spare connection hoses was left lying on the ground with the drain cock open. The oil was transported at a warm temperature to make it more liquid and to enable it to be pumped easily from the train. Unfortunately, this made it run like water over a large area including the Up Goods, Up Main, banker sidings, oil yard sidings and all the way down to our "Mess" cabin. (NOTE; It will be interesting to see if they find residue when they dig the foundations for the new station).

The following night, workmen spent all night dumping 400 tons of sand on the slick. Several months were taken cleaning up the oil which including lifting the Up Goods line to dig out the sand and oil with a JCB. On Sunday 4th January I was again booked with Pat, with D7021 on "an oil slick special" 08.00 to 17.20. This included several "GRAMPUS" wagons one of which had a JCB in it. A number of us had our shoes ruined from walking in all the oil and we claimed for a new pair and were paid in full.

In 1970 one of our Hymeks was used in a test but this was not on the Lickey Bank but on Garringtons Bank. Fred Bourne was the driver and Darryl Lucas his mate when accompanied by Inspector Alan Jones they ventured over the bridge and almost into the works. Darryl says "I remember we had to proceed with extreme caution over their sidings and over the bridge. We were then required to stand on the bridge for a few minutes and then clear the bridge on the works side." As far as anyone can remember the test was a success but no more was heard about it and we eventually lost the Garringtons traffic to road.

Another Oil Leak

Why is Darryl always involved in oil leaks? Here he tells of another incident in 1970 when he was my mate:

One of the incidents of a main fuel pipe leak occurred on Saturday 8th August 1970 at around 22.30. The loco involved was D7023. At around 21.30 our locos were standing at the coal stage and we were in the mess room chatting. A change of engine tone on our loco ticking over outside seemed unusual and so we went to investigate.

We went outside to see (glistening in the lights of the stage) something coming out of a number of the engine room vents and running down the side of the loco. We at first thought that it was oil but upon entering the engine room, there was a strong smell of diesel oil and a thick mist throughout.

Further investigation revealed the diesel fuel was being sprayed at extremely high pressure from a split in one of the main copper fuel pipes. This was being sprayed all over the wall of the engine room and was all over the floor. Pat quickly shut down the engine while I went to find some rags to mop up the fuel. With the flow of fuel now stopped, we dried the pipe thoroughly and considered the situation. It was found that there was a split in the pipe around one and a half inches long. It was obvious that we would need to seal the split with a temporary repair of some type.

All drivers were supplied with a basic emergency kit which included a roll of PVC electrical insulating tape. I went to get my toolbox from the car. It was obvious that the PVC insulating tape would stretch under the high pressure and would not work. I therefore searched through my toolbox and found a roll of the old type of non stretch electrical insulating tape and some bare copper wire. We wrapped two layers of PVC tape tightly round the pipe followed by three layers of the non -stretch type. This was followed by another two layers of PVC and each end of the repair was tightly clamped with two twists of copper wire. We didn't think for a minute that this would work but when we turned on the power and pressed the start button, Hey presto, there was not the slightest sign of a leak.

Pat rang the fitters at Worcester who told us to try to get the loco to Worcester depot where they would either try to make a repair or replace our loco. Upon our arrival, we followed the fitters into the engine room to see if our repair was still holding and were surprised to find that there was still absolutely no sign of a leak. The fitters were very complimentary on our temporary repair and said that they couldn't have done better themselves. We were given D7021 as a replacement loco and returned home feeling pretty pleased with ourselves.

In August 1971 I was involved in an incident at Blackwell. It was a Friday night at 23-30 and we had just banked a cement train with 7025 and 7021 in multiple. Mick Wood was my mate and as we dropped back from the train Mick shouted hold tight as he spotted sparks as the train suddenly came to a stand. We couldn't avoid hitting the back of the train and knocking our right hand buffer off. The train driver came back to us and apologised saying that he had taken his foot off the deadmans. The guard was unhurt but a little bit shaken as he had been asleep and ended up on the floor of the brake van.

We eventually lost our regular engines and most of the Hymeks were used for banking at one time or another. Diesel hydraulics were out of fashion though and were gradually being withdrawn and so the writing was on the cards for our Hymeks and on October 23rd 1972 6910 arrived at Bromsgrove so we could all have a week's training. The Hymeks had gone by November 5th and 6603 and 6986 were in residence.

Roster from 1-2-1972

Sunday	Monday	Tuesday	Wednesday	Thursday	Friday	Saturday
08-05	08-05 S	08-05 S	08-05 S	08-05 S	08-05 S	RD
	RD	16-05 M	16-05 M	16-05 M	16-05 M	16-05 M
	RD	00-05 S	00-05 S	00-05 S	00-05 S	00-05 M
00-05	12-05 Spare	12-05 Spare	12-05 Spare	12-05 Spare	12-05 Spare	RD
	16-05 S	16-05 S	16-05 S	16-05 S	16-05 S	RD
	00-05 M	00-05 M	00-05 M	00-05 M	00-05 M	RD
16-05	16-05 M	Spare	08-05 M	08-00 Spare	08-00 Spare	RD
	08-05 M	08-05 M	RD	08-05 M	08-05 M	08-05 M

S= Single loco. M= Two engines in multiple.

By the following year the single engine had been taken out and we lost some more of our men to Garringtons and the Austin. It was soon found that another engine was required at busy times and so an engine would be sent up from Worcester at 21-00 to help out until 03-20.

Sometimes two 37's weren't available and another class of engine would be sent to work in tandem and on the odd occasion no engine was available at all and a single engine had to suffice. If we were assisting on the main line any combination could be sent to do the banking while we were away or the engine that had arrived on the tanks in the yard would be asked to help out. On November 7th 1973 Class 31 number 5826 worked with 6998 for the day.

On one occasion a class 46 number 46034 was sent up for banking before someone realised that they were not suitable.

An accident occurred at Bromsgrove on February 6th 1974 when 5690 arrived on the up goods. Some wagons were left while others were put off in the sidings but these rolled back into the bank engine siding and demolished the stop block. Luckily the bankers, 6862 and 6903, were up the bank at the time. On 21st June 1974 bank engines 37234 and 25154 were away assisting 40180 on a train to Gloucester and Worcester sent up a class 47 to do the banking.

One of the young enthusiasts who would often be at the South was Robert Dunn and on March 4 1973 I took him and his friend Terry Franks down to Westbury to see ex Bromsgrove man Philip Marshman with a view to getting Bob a job on the railway when he left school in 1975. I had met Robert some years before as I knew his dad through our shared love of gardening and had been invited to the house to see Robert's new model railway. Despite having an interview at Bristol and passing a test the job at Westbury didn't come off as the hostel where Bob was going to stay was closed down and Howard Griffiths and I made some phone calls to try to get him fixed up elsewhere. Eventually Bob started training at Saltley but when a vacancy occurred at Bromsgrove he transferred here booking on for the first time on Tuesday June 17th 1975. Bob was given three days to familiarise himself with the depot and had his first proper turn on the 16-05 shift with Sid Wheeley on the Friday. By this time we had two 37's in multiple after having almost a year of class 25/37 banking in multiple. This had started after 7511 was sent up for trials with 6974 on February 13 1974. The trial was a success and 7577 arrived for crew training in April. We had a week's training on the class and on May 6 7577 and 37217 began work. We had all sorts of problems with this combination and tried them with the 37 leading and then the 25 leading when they sometimes didn't want to work together. 25161 failed on May 15th 1974 while working with 37217 and with no replacement available the 37 had to carry on alone. The following day 47 number 1655 was sent up to work in tandem.

Two bankers were not always enough for some trains especially if two 25's were working in multiple as on August 6th 1974. An oil train needed three bankers when it arrived at Bromsgrove behind 47530 and 31117 was sent up from Worcester to help. Eventually in April 1975 we went back to a pair of 37's with relief all round.

Fred and Bob had a taste of express work when they were in Worcester for refuelling on July 21st 1975. They were enjoying a quiet lunch in the canteen when a fitter appeared and asked them to assist 46037 on the 11-40 Bristol to Manchester which had failed in the station. A dash was made over to the shed to collect 37210 and 236 and off they went to New Street, Bankers to the rescue again.

On Sunday September 14 1975 1E50 headed by 45143 was suffering from loss of power and Fred Bourne and Bob Dunn hooked on the front with 37223 and 37292 and worked the train of 12 coaches to New St. The Peak was deposited on Saltley shed before the bankers returned home.

Howard Griffiths was another one to leave us around 1975/6 when after four years he moved back to Worcester before heading for Merseyside and after training on the electrics became a driver at Kirkdale.

Sometimes a train would fail on the bank with another train behind it; this was the case on October 26th. An express with 12 coaches had slipped to a stand on the leaves near the top of the bank. Another express was following and it too had slipped to a stand so the lone banker 37214 was summoned to assist. The first express was got underway and pushed to the rear of the other before the whole lot got underway and made it safely to the top. The following day the Bristol-Newcastle mail 1E38 stuck at Pikes Pool and the following train 6E67 Bristol-York Dringhouses attempted to push it without success. The resident bankers 37214 and 37305 together with the Worcester class 47 number 47182 went to the rescue and pushed the lot up to Blackwell.

All this passenger work had made Bob Dunn yearn for more and in March 1976 he left to further his career at Saltley. This was not the last we saw of him though as he would often pass through. He actually stopped to speak to us on one occasion late in 1976. I was banking 8E38 Cardiff-Tinsley with Mick Wood as my mate when the train engine slipped to a stand when it encountered the leaves near the top of the bank. Bob was secondman on the train engine and walked back to speak with us. The Worcester banker was on its way and together we gave Bob a good shove to Blackwell.

It often seemed the case that when a train stuck there was another one behind and this happened again on 29th November 1977 when 47499 stopped just short of Blackwell with the 21-10 Bristol to Edinburgh. It was pushed over the top by the following parcels train and the two bankers.

In 1979 Mick Wood was passed for driving and this gave me more flexibility with the rostering. After Mick it was the turn of Kevin Barham and we were then all able to take a driving turn. Mick and Kevin did their training at Saltley and were passed out on a class 47 this was handy as when we were at Gloucester and a 37 was not available they would often ask what other traction we knew and if Kevin or Mick was with me we could take a 47.

Mick remembers an incident when he was driving and after banking a train it came to a stand at Blackwell. After a few minutes the train driver, a Derby man, appeared and said he had stopped so the banker could be uncoupled. When banking a train the signals would return to danger before we passed them so to stop hearing the warning all the time we would isolate the AWS when banking. If we were going anywhere other than Blackwell we would of course have it in operation. Someone must have shopped us as one day an inspector appeared and asked us about it. He was just doing his job of course and could see our point of view but asked us to use AWS whenever there was anyone else around.

We carried on like this for the next few years with a combination of banking regular trains, assisting trains that got stuck on the bank and taking over failures. On 17th May 1980 45062 failed and was assisted to New St by 37224 and 37242. Things were about to change though and the following year HST's started regular workings up and down the bank. Changes to our workings also occurred and we took our engines to Gloucester around mid-day on a Saturday and didn't resume until the Monday so our wages dropped considerably as we had been working three Sundays out of nine for many years. I think it was at this time that Sid

Wheeley took early retirement. Before Sid left I think he and Mick were the first to assist an HST which turned out to be a bit of a shambles. With two engines perhaps it was thought that they would never need assistance and we never had any training in the coupling up procedure, the driver didn't seem to know a lot about it either and someone from the Buffet came to help. The bankers coupled up in a fashion but something was not right with the pin and when they went over the top at Blackwell they felt a bump and on examination found the bar had bent the cowling. Eventually the mistake was found and put right before they continued on their way to New Street. There was an inquiry into this incident but I don't remember the outcome.

*　*　*　*　*

Assisting an HST on one occasion the bankers ran past a signal at Kings Norton, the HST driver had not isolated his brake and in the rush the banker didn't do a brake test so that was something to remember for the future. With a loco hauled train assistance was usually provided at the front but if it was not possible then we sometimes propelled from the rear providing the front driver had control of the brake and I think there was a restriction of speed to 40mph.

When trains came to grief on the leaves near the top of the bank and there was a train following they would try and assist but this invariably failed and we would be called for. I remember one occasion when a DMU was behind an express and of course he stood no chance and we were called to push them both.

There was a lot of excitement and plenty of delays when what I think was a class 45 caught fire down at Stoke Works. This was possibly around 1984/5 and the bankers were summoned to Stoke to take the engine off. Arriving at Bromsgrove with the engine pouring with smoke Mick Wood got on the phone at signal G18 to get instructions and was surprised when Gloucester told him to put the engine in the oil depot. Mick quickly explained that it would not be a good idea to put an engine that was on fire in an oil terminal and so the engine was deposited in the banker spur at the south. Returning to the station the bankers then dashed down to Stoke to collect the train and take it to Birmingham. In the meantime the fire brigade had been running around looking for the train that was on fire firstly at Stoke and then Newton Bridge where they spotted smoke coming from the loco and went down Garringtons car park to deal with the fire. I don't know whether there were any flames but there was plenty of black smoke as it was the batteries that had overheated.

On 2nd July 1985 with Mick Wood as my mate we were asked to assist an HST, 43143 leading and 43019 on the rear, to New St. We had got the hang of coupling up by now and so were soon ready to go. Mick was driving and the guard was informed that we would start off and then conduct a brake test and perhaps he should tell his passengers of what was about to happen, which he duly did. It was unfortunate that he didn't heed the message himself as he was looking out of the door, which was open, as we did the test. When Mick looked back there was the guard dusting himself down at the side of the track having fallen out of the train. Luckily he didn't hurt himself too much, just his pride, and we were soon under way.

Accident at Eckington

Sometime after 1979 when Mick Wood was my mate we had a frightening experience when we were travelling to Gloucester for refuelling. We had two class 37's in multiple and Mick was taking a turn at driving as by this time he had passed out as a driver. It was in the daytime and visibility was good. As we approached the occupation crossing before Eckington loop we sounded the horn as we approached the whistle board and then a car suddenly appeared on the crossing in front of us. Mick made an emergency brake application but we had no chance of stopping. We came to a stop between the crossing and the signal and I immediately went to the signal to get all trains stopped. While I was doing this Mick walked back to see what he could do for the driver and I joined him after speaking to Gloucester Box. We were relieved to find the driver still alive especially after seeing that the car was now in two pieces. When we collided the car hit a platelayers hut before bouncing off that and ending up in a field. By the time I arrived at the scene some local residents from the nearby houses had come out to see what had happened and we were informed that an ambulance was on its way. The driver was a lady and I think she got away with a broken shoulder and pelvis. Inspection of our engines, the leading one of which had a small snowplough, revealed that all we had was an air pipe that had been torn off. When we arrived at Gloucester we were met by the police and made statements and Keith Bignall, the area manager came to see us and asked if we were alright to drive back. When we answered in the affirmative he gave us five pounds to have a drink later. As we passed the sight of the accident on our return the television cameras were there and we were shown passing on the TV that evening. Apart from an incident at Blackwell this was the only other accident which I was involved in with diesels.

Since we were down to just the two engines in multiple we started to make things easy for ourselves by eliminating the need to change engines at Blackwell. One of us would drive the lead engine with the other man in the rear cab of the second one. At Blackwell the man on the second engine would take control for the return to Bromsgrove.

The class 37's were pretty reliable engines but there was an occasion when I think Alan Price was my mate. Alan was driving the lead engine and I was in the rear cab of the other engine ready to drive back to Bromsgrove. We got away ok and picked up speed through the station but when we got on the bank the speed dropped off dramatically. My engine was flat out and I assumed the other was doing the same but it took nearly half an hour to get to Blackwell. On the return we stopped at the signal at the bottom of the bank and my mate appeared to tell me the reason for our slow progress up the bank. The lead engine had run low on coolant and had shut down. A glance at the repair book showed there had been a problem with the radiator and so when we got to the south we used the mop bucket to get water to the engine where we pumped it into the system. With the system filled the engine was able to be started and we went to Gloucester to get it changed. I think Alan Price, a local lad, later transferred to Gloucester as he was gone by the time the depot closed.

In the 1980s traffic dropped off a bit and rumours started that the depot would close but we had been hearing rumours for years, ever since dieselisation, so we didn't worry too much. I was hoping to reach retirement on the railway but the news finally arrived in 1986 that the depot would close at the end of the summer timetable and any banking requirements would be met from Gloucester.

Last Day

ON THE final day, 26th September a reporter from the local paper arrived to interview us and take our photo. There were only five of us left by now, two sets and one man spare but Ken Suckling declined to come for the photo. Only a single engine was at Bromsgrove for my last shift as Gloucester men had come up and exchanged the pair for just one engine. The engine 37177 was parked down below the bridge and Mick went down to bring it up for the photo. A young enthusiast by the name of Neil Gordon who was often at the South had made a headboard for the last day and he accompanied Mick and fitted the headboard before bringing the loco up. The photographer liked the headboard and so it was removed and held by us all for the photo. I was on the afternoon shift with Kevin Barham later relieved by Mick Wood who booked on for his final shift at 22-55. Mick was accompanied by Gloucester man Dave Hinett. Dave was standing in for Ken who had some time owing to him. With the formalities over we prepared to go to Gloucester to collect another engine. My mate, who was not normally very keen on having visitors on the engine suggested that Neil and Chris Howse who was another regular at the South have a ride to Gloucester with us as it would be their last opportunity.

So about an hour after booking on the four of us set off south with the headboard proudly displayed on the engine, as we passed through Cheltenham Neil and Chris ducked down so as not to be seen. Approaching Gloucester I sent them back into the engine room where they waited with their hands over their ears while we attached the other engine, 37501. We were about forty five minutes on shed and before we left I transferred the headboard to the front for the trip home. Our passengers came back in the cab when we got under way again. At Cheltenham we were stopped in the platform and with a lot of passengers waiting there many crowded round the engine to look at the Lickey Banker headboard, time for the lads to keep out of sight again. We arrived back at Bromsgrove at 18-39 ready to bank our last few trains.

We had quite a few visitors during this last evening and a number had a ride up the bank. I'm not sure how many trips we did but 47112 on 4E88 was one we banked at 20-05 and my last one was when we banked 47003 with 6E64 at 21-40. I think Neil removed the headboard after banking this train and took it home for safe keeping before returning to take his last photographs.

Kevin and I were relieved by Mick and Dave who banked 47544 on the sleeper 1S19 at 23-01. I hung around to have a chat with Mick but had a bit of a wait as after the sleeper they had a freight to bank, a class 47 on 7E95 at 23-20. After I went home a number of trains were banked during the early hours before the engines were taken to Worcester for the final time. Mick returned to Bromsgrove on the bus and that was it after more than 146 years of banking by Bromsgrove men.

End

So there we are. On the final day in 1986 when interviewed by a local reporter I said I might write a book, this is it. I should have done it earlier while things were fresh in my memory but better late than never. If you have read this far then perhaps I have not made too bad a job of it and maybe you have even enjoyed it. I have tried to mention everyone I worked with as it was the men that made the depot what it was and if it was a bit repetitive in places I make no apology for that.

Best Wishes Pat